Benjamin D. Scott

George Hedley

Born in Tientsin, China, George Hedley took his preparatory work at Ashville College, Harrogate, England. He received his B.A., M.A., and B.D. from the University of Southern California and his D. Theol. from the Pacific School of Religion.

Dr. Hedley taught at the College of Puget Sound, the Pacific School of Religion, and Hartford Seminary Foundation before going to Mills College where he is now Professor of Economics and Sociology and Chaplain of the College.

How Can We Be Christian on Campus?
Can One Be Scholarly about Religion?
What Is the Chief End of Man?
What Is the Meaning of Prayer? What Does One Pray for?

Students, parents, and indeed everyone interested in the religious development of American youth will want to read this wise and honest book.

Religion on the Campus

A frank appraisal of religion in college life...

The college youth of today are constantly facing new ideas, testing old beliefs against new sets of values. Invariably, the religion of their childhood must be re-thought in the light of new learning. As Chaplain of Mills College, George Hedley is keenly aware of both the problems and the rewards which this situation can bring. In this collection of twenty-two sermons delivered at Mills, he shows how the quest for learning can be applied to religion, so that a student can graduate with a mature, firm faith.

The directness, humor, and depth of understanding which made his previous books so popular are again evident in this frank study. Dr. Hedley explains the relationship of religion to other college activities, including the social as well as the scholarly, showing how the information gained from courses in science and human relations can support rather than diminish religious faith. With a clear understanding of the student's personal problems he answers such questions as:

By GEORGE HEDLEY

THE SYMBOL OF THE FAITH
A Study of the Apostles' Creed
THE CHRISTIAN HERITAGE IN AMERICA
THE SUPERSTITIONS OF THE IRRELIGIOUS
CHRISTIAN WORSHIP
Some Meanings and Means
RELIGION ON THE CAMPUS
*Some Sermons in the Chapel
of Mills College*

Some Sermons
in the Chapel of Mills College

Religion on the Campus

By GEORGE HEDLEY, 1899

New York
THE MACMILLAN COMPANY
1955

Grateful acknowledgment is made to the following publishers:

The Clarendon Press, Oxford, for permission to quote from *The Testament of Beauty* by Robert Bridges.

Doubleday & Company, Inc., New York, for permission to quote from *the lives and times of archy and mehitabel* by Don Marquis, copyright, 1927, by Doubleday & Company, Inc.

Preface

There were sixteen of us sharing in the Holy Communion this morning at seven o'clock. That is one illustration of "Religion on the Campus," and perhaps a more valid and vital one than any sermon can be. There were 1,322 individual communions (more than twice the total number of our student body) at ninety celebrations in the Chapel during the academic year 1953–1954. To my mind that matters more than all the sermons put together.

In our effort to express and to live religion, however, it is inevitable that sometimes we shall want to discuss it. The first group of sermons here assembled, after an introductory chat with Freshmen, were an effort to say something of what religion is, might be, ought to be, in a liberal arts college with a Christian heritage. Next are reproduced replies to questions about some specific campus and student problems. The third major section reflects the very lively concern of students of today with basic issues of theology. Finally, there is a brief valedictory to departing Seniors.

One of the scripts, that on prayer, belongs to the year 1952–1953. (There will be another treatment of that problem next Sunday, but I have decided to use the earlier one as being somewhat more inclusive.) The discussions of Christian marriage and of atheism are of this current year 1954–1955. All the rest were products of the academic year preceding, 1953–1954, and constitute just about half of that year's total sermon material.

These are sermons written for oral presentation, and I have not thought it fitting to try to turn them into essays. Local and temporary references have been omitted or generalized in those

v

cases where they would have meaning only for our immediate campus family. Others, which carry their own interpretation within them, have been allowed to stand. Names of students who raised particular questions appear without disguise, as a small but sincere tribute to those who have rendered special service in driving us to think.

I owe to these students and to many others, to faculty colleagues and especially to members of our residence staff, hearty thanks both for general intellectual provocation and spiritual challenge, and for the direct suggestion that some of the materials should be brought together in convenient and fairly lasting form. I wish to thank also the Reverend Dr. Raymond F. McLain, who at the time of this writing is General Director of the Commission on Christian Higher Education of the National Council of Churches, for friendly encouragement in the project.

Grateful acknowledgments are made to the Clarendon Press, Oxford, for permission to reprint eight lines from *The Testament of Beauty*, by Robert Bridges, and to Messrs. Doubleday & Company for allowing me to use fifteen lines from "the lesson of the moth" in Don Marquis's *archy and mehitabel*.

The reader will note that with each sermon are shown the Biblical materials that were read in the given service. These always are relevant, and in many cases their reading is essential as background for the discussion. Hymns and prayers also were chosen with reference to the theme of the day, the former with special discernment by our student choir directors Marilyn Feller, Virginia (Nikki) Tenneson, and Nancy Franz. I thank them too, and the choir which they have so ably led.

It is tempting to launch here into a detailed account of our Chapel's life and work at Mills, and into a general discussion of religion as a dynamic on the college campus. But what is here, and what we believe ought to be, will (I trust) appear with sufficient clarity in the pages that follow. For fifteen years it has been my high privilege to live in an atmosphere at once of active religious inquiry and of sincere religious devotion, created and maintained by students and faculty alike. For that I am grateful, to these people and to the God whom they seek and try to serve. What more can I say?

G. H.

Ruddigore
Mills College
St. Andrew's Day 1954

Contents

SOME QUESTIONS OF THEOLOGY

CONCLUDING: FOR SENIORS

INTRODUCTORY: FOR FRESHMEN

A Cloak, Some Books, and the Parchments

A Cloak, Some Books, and the Parchments

20 September 1953, at the Sunday morning service in Freshman Orientation Week. Psalm 145: 1–10; II Timothy 4: 1–18.

*   *   *

The cloke that I left at Troas with Carpus, when thou comest, bring with thee, and the books, but especially the parchments.—II Timothy 4:13.

The text stands in a highly personal note from an old man to a young friend of his: one of those amazingly human bits that keep reminding us how real and human the writers of the Bible and their first readers were. I'll confess now that probably I'm going to overpress the meaning of the text in order to serve our present purpose. But it does vividly suggest some things that were important to St. Paul and his protégé Timothy, and that I believe still are important to old men and young people these nineteen hundred years later.

For something like ten or fifteen years the apostle Paul had been traveling on the Mediterranean Sea and around its shores: preaching, debating, organizing churches, advising and disputing with churches he had organized earlier, getting into prison and out again, surviving shipwrecks, writing letters, working out the beginnings of a Christian theology, contending with ailments that may have included both malaria and poor eyesight. Now, after yet another imprisonment, and what was at least his fourth ex-

3

perience of shipwreck, he was almost at the end of the road. Under house arrest in Rome, awaiting the outcome of his appeal to the Emperor Nero, he wrote out of the lonely quiet to the boy who had been his associate and secretary in the years just past.

Probably almost all of what we call the first epistle to Timothy, and a large part of the second, were written by someone other than Paul long after the apostle himself had died. But the bulk of the fourth and last chapter, in this second letter, rings true both to St. Paul's personality and to his situation. He reflects on the good fight he has fought, and he recognizes that he has finished his course. He seems to be annoyed with Demas, who has gone off to northern Greece, and perhaps also with Crescens and Titus, who respectively are in what we know today as Turkey and Yugoslavia. He is still angry with one Alexander the coppersmith, though we do not find out exactly why. (Someone has suggested that perhaps it was because already there were too many pennies on the collection plates.)

Lonely and tired, the old fighter and missionary looks forward to Timothy's coming to Rome; and he asks him to bring some necessary supplies with him. In his busyness, and his concentration upon his work, the apostle may have developed some of the habits of the absent-minded professor. It appears that when he ended a visit with his friend Carpus in Troas (which is the ancient Troy), he left his cloak there. It can be pretty chilly in Rome in the winter, and that cloak would help now. He wants also his books, for his mind has not yet lost its driving energy; but especially he wants to be sure of getting the parchments, which are the scrolls of the Hebrew scriptures.

All that was long ago and far away. St. Paul was an old man at the end of his career, and you are young women at the beginning of yours. What relevance can this little item have for us this morning? I warned you that I might overplay the interpretation a bit. But when I was thinking toward this first Sunday service of the academic year, my mind kept turning back to the simple request for supplies that the old man made, and to what seemed to me to be a reasonable series of inferences from it for ourselves. What can you and I read in St. Paul's lines, and between them?

First of all he mentions the cloak. No doubt his concern was chiefly for keeping warm: I don't imagine he cared one way or the other about looking fashionable. For you, however, a cloak (or a coat, or a jacket, or a mink, or whatever) has at least a dual meaning. Its function is in part practical, and related to the weather. I have noticed, however, that the weather very often takes a second place with young women, who readily will suffocate in furs on a hot day, or shiver in a formal on a winter's evening, if only they can be sure they're wearing "the right thing" and making a sufficient impression.

On neither count am I anxious now to quarrel with you. The point I want to suggest is rather a positive one. It is that physical and material concerns do matter in our life, and that they warrant a fair share of our conscious attention. The College does its best to keep you warm and well fed: though you will learn soon, if you don't know already, that our campus heating system has some quaint vagaries of its own; and, despite all the dietetics staff can do, there will be some meals that won't suit your taste, and some dishes cooked otherwise than Mother used to cook them. The Department of Health, Physical Education, and Recreation also exists in large part to keep you fit in body, and thus equal to the heavy demands upon your energy that your college life inevitably will make.

For the rest, you'll settle down to settling your clothes problems for yourself, with due respect, of course, to the pressures of campus fashion. That means you'll look pretty tacky from Monday morning to Friday afternoon, and then emerge from the shabby weekday chrysalis into a weekend splendor of suits and hats, of dresses and cloaks, of make-up and hair styling, which will make you literally unrecognizable to your nearsighted professors. And that's all right too, both in the practicality of classroom wear and in the happy impracticality of your out-on-the-town attire.

We are complete people, and to maintain our completeness we must give to these physical aspects of life their full and proper place. You need to feel well and be well. You need to be comfortable. As young women you unquestionably need to look smart, anyway some of the time. I offer you St. Paul's cloak, then, both to keep you warm and to make you handsome. This is important in your life, and you ought to pay attention to it.

But St. Paul wanted some other things too. The books come next; and we can see these as representing the dominant intellectual concerns of college work. Paul himself was an educated man, trained in the graduate school of theology in Jerusalem under the great Jewish scholar the Rabbi Gamaliel I. Paul seems also to have had more than a passing acquaintance with the Greek culture that prevailed in his home town of Tarsus in Asia Minor. All his life his mind remained alert and his thinking vigorous; and even now, in the twilight of his days, we find him still demanding his books so that he still can go on learning.

Books are going to bulk largely in your lives for these next few years. You can't think to avoid them, in view of the demands we of the faculty will lay upon you. The real question is whether you are going to regard the books just as tiresome, though inescapable, acquaintances, or as real friends whose company you eagerly will seek.

The library is full of books that can be your friends indeed: friends that can enlighten you, encourage you, amuse you, straighten you out when you're confused, strengthen you for the whole job of living. Your eyesight is a lot better than Paul's was, and your range of possible reading is infinitely wider. What remains is for you to catch the eager interest of the apostle, and of everyone who has made intellectual headway for himself and has given intellectual leadership to others. Get hold of the books, then. Keep your minds at work. That is why you're here.

But body and mind, the physical and the intellectual, are not all of life. The third thing Timothy was to bring with him, and the one marked off by "but especially," was the collection of parchments. These, as I have said, were the scrolls of the Hebrew scriptures: what we call the Old Testament, which was all the Bible there was till Paul himself began to write more of it in these letters of his. The parchments stand thus for the area of spiritual awareness, the region of moral obligation, the world of religious value.

This above all the old man knew he needed, and this above all you and I need too. Facing the autocratic power of Nero Caesar, living under the overwhelming might of the massive Roman Empire, meeting the arguments and cavils of a highly articulate and acutely critical Greek civilization, St. Paul turned again and again to the ancient writings of his ancient faith. Here alone could he find a world view that included all of the problems, a line of action that would make his living coherent and complete, a poise of spirit sufficient to carry him through the confusions and the struggles in which every day he found himself.

"I couldn't find no way on earth to gain peace of mind," says a song that has had a vast juke-box and radio popularity. There is a way, if not to peace of mind, at least to stability of soul: and that is much the greater good. Our world is even more complex than was St. Paul's, and our confusions certainly are no less. We need to think clearly, and the books will help us on this. We need also to believe vitally and to live bravely; and this is where the parchments, the values that belong to religion, are essential for our sanity and our success. That is why Mills College has a Chapel, and that is why the Chapel invites you to share in its continuing life.

As we go on to examine the subject of "Religion on the Campus," we shall be trying in considerable detail to decide what religion is, what it can do for us, and what we can do and be as religious persons. The basic proposition is simply that just as we need sound and well clothed bodies, and sound and well informed minds, so also we need a sound and well tested scheme of ultimate value: which is to say, a sound and well tested religion. A better poet than the song lyricist has written of

> A central peace, subsisting at the heart
> Of endless agitation.

This is what every one of us today needs most of all. This is what a real and living religion can give us all.

Take the cloak, then. Look well in it, and feel comfortable. Get the books, and get out of them all that they can provide. And remember always that you need the parchments too: but especially, but definitely.

RELIGION ON THE CAMPUS

Religion and Scholarship

Religion and the Fine Arts

Religion and the Natural Sciences

Religion and Community Service

Religion and the Humanities

Religion MTWThFS

Religion and Scholarship

27 September 1953. Psalm 119:17–24; Proverbs 9:1–12;
I Peter 3:8–17.

* * *

*The fear of the Lord is the beginning of wisdom: and the
knowledge of the holy is understanding.*—Proverbs 9:10.

*Be ready always to give an answer to every man that asketh
you a reason of the hope that is in you.*—I Peter 3:15.

One of our interesting little campus institutions is that which
is called the "faculty colloquium." Three or four times a year
individual members of the faculty, who are engaged in some
particular line of research in their own fields, report to their
colleagues on what they are doing, and on what they have found
out or hope to find out. Whenever I have attended (and I always
do when I can) I have profited greatly. I've picked up a little
information, from time to time, about Peruvian poetry and Pacific
shellfish and the growth of cancers, about steam engines on
American farms, and Jack London's dealings with his publishers,
and shrubs of the California Sierra. Always I am staggered by
the amount of knowledge some of my friends possess in fields
of which I know exactly nothing; and always I learn, if not a
thoroughgoing lesson in subject matter, at least a thoroughly
healthy one in intellectual humility.

As it must to all men, the duty of making such a report has
come a couple of times to me. On the first occasion I had been
working on the history and meaning of the Apostles' Creed; and
I tried to tell my colleagues something of the way in which that

11

Christian formula can be traced back from its present, sixth century phrasing to a briefer version which was current in the fourth century after Christ, and then to various of its constituent parts in the writings of the Church Fathers as early as the beginning of the second century. The evidence is on the whole very specific, and the conclusions to be drawn from it are fairly clear; and it was on literary evidence and critical judgments, rather than on the content of the Christian faith itself, that I laid my major emphasis that afternoon.

The chairman was a professor of biology who, I'm pretty sure, wouldn't have been present to hear about the Creed if it had not been his assigned duty to preside. As I was speaking, I noticed on his face an expression that seemed to me to betray at once growing interest and no little of bewilderment. When I had finished, he came up at once and shook my hand. "George," he said, "I had no idea it was possible to be scientific about religion."

The specific question of the relationship of religion to the natural sciences as such is going to engage our attention soon. But this biologist's view, to the effect that religion and science could have nothing to do with each other, represents the whole problem of what religion and scholarship have to do with each other; and his negative assumption undeniably reflects the thinking and the attitudes of many people, perhaps of most, who are involved in college and university life today. Has religion any proper place in academic life? Can one be scholarly about religion? Can a scholarly person be genuinely and sincerely religious? These are some of the questions every scholar, every student, and every religious person needs to face squarely and honestly.

The organization of our Mills curriculum in terms of four major schools within the College provides a neat and ready-made outline for the inquiry. In the setting of the sacred drama of the Holy Communion we may inquire into the relations of "Religion and the Fine Arts." Next, in a fairly sharp contrast, we shall turn our attention directly to the problem of "Religion and the

Natural Sciences." With the whole college community involved in the campaign for the World University Service fund, it will be fitting for us to think about "Religion and Community Service." Then comes the question of "Religion and the Humanities": and it is worth noting that it is in the School of Humanities that our Department of Philosophy and Religion is classified. Finally in this sequence we shall examine the place of religion in our daily life on campus, under the Record Office terminology of "Religion MTWThFS."

In this general introductory survey let us ask ourselves first what we may think to be the right relationship (or whether there can be any right relationship) between religious faith and scholarly inquiry. In the United States we have two major and quite different academic traditions on this point, and we at Mills don't quite belong to either. On the one hand there are the great public institutions, generally state universities and colleges, in most of which religion has no place either in the course of study or in the official interests of the administration. On the other, there are the numerous smaller colleges which were founded by particular religious denominations, in part for the training of their clergy and in part for the indoctrination of laymen and laywomen so that they would keep on being loyal adherents of the given Church.

The church-related colleges are the older, and are represented by practically all of the famous academic foundations of the seventeenth and eighteenth centuries. It was not until the nineteenth that the state university became a familiar type, and scarcely till the twentieth that it reached its present place of dominance. In some cases the church colleges have maintained much of their original character, still having required courses in Bible and required attendance at frequent chapel services. In more, however, the hold of the Church has been gradually loosened, until there is either no legal control by the denomination at all, or such a slight connection that the difference between the church school and the state one would be invisible to the casual observer.

Mills properly belongs to neither of these major patterns in American higher education. It always has been a private institution, never a church-connected one. At the same time it is specifically and vigorously a Christian institution. The will of Cyrus Taggart Mills, written in 1884, provided that the trustees should keep this College "for ever thoroughly Christian, but not sectarian." How well this purpose has been and is being fulfilled is for the Mills girls of each succeeding college generation to judge. That the objective is a sound one I am fully convinced; and that Christianity and scholarship do thus belong together I profoundly believe.

But there is no denying that the weight of academic opinion in this country is against me. The deliberate disregard of religion in the state universities, the fading out of recognizable religion in so many of the church-founded colleges, the distrust of religion by thousands of faculty members in schools of every kind, would seem to lay the burden of proof on us who claim that we can be scholarly and religious at one and the same time, religious and scholarly in one and the same person. It follows that we must not only assert our point, but also argue it.

Can one be scientific, or scholarly, about religion? My friend the biologist had supposed not; and he was speaking for a multitude of others who think the same way. Yet I will contend that there is much about religion that is susceptible to just the same kind of factual inquiry, just the same kind of critical analysis, just the same kind of logical discussion as belongs to any other field of human interest and activity. I will say further that the inquiries have been made, the analyses worked out, the discussions carried on, at the highest levels of sober and objective study: and precisely by religious people. If anyone today doesn't know this, he simply convicts himself of not being scholarly enough to have asked what is going on outside his own field of specialization.

The external facts of religious history and religious life not only permit, but also demand, the most careful and critical examining and identifying. Thus, for example, the books of the Bible have been studied in the light both of what they say themselves, and of what can be learned about them from supplementary evidence that comes from the various times of their writing. Out of this study, which has been carried on even from the earliest days, but which has had its greatest development in this past century and a half—just the period, you will notice, in which all our other academic disciplines have been growing into their present forms—out of this study have come certain conclusions which are as standard, and as thoroughly established, as is any hypothesis in secular history or general literature, and definitely more so than are most of the current formulations of sociologists, economists, and psychologists.

The regular courses in the literature of the Bible will introduce you to many of these established findings. Among them are the knowledge that the first five books of the Old Testament were not written by Moses, nor by any other one man, but are elaborate composites whose materials date from the ninth century B.C. all the way down to the fourth; the knowledge (and I stress that word again) that King David wrote few if any of the Psalms, and that our present book of Psalms includes some poems written as late as the second century B.C.; the knowledge that our four Gospels in their present forms are not independent, eyewitness accounts of the life and teaching of Jesus, but second-generation Christian products greatly conditioned by the life and thought of the early Church, and in literary terms reflecting the story of an extremely involved interdependence; and the knowledge (once more) that of the fourteen letters commonly supposed to have been written by St. Paul, not more than nine actually are from his hand.

All this is very complicated, and to those who have not ventured before into the field of Biblical scholarship it may seem a bit shocking. Nevertheless it is the product of careful research and discriminating judgment, and it ranks as highly in its own area as do the evolutionary hypothesis in biology and the Einsteinian equations in physics. Any university, then, which ignores this aspect of human learning is not a complete university, and any college which leaves it out of the curriculum is not a total college of the liberal arts. Rigorous scholarship ought to be applied to religion. It can be. It has been. The true scholar in any field will acquaint himself with these facts, and for ever will cease to discount the work which his colleagues in religion have done in their discipline while he has been carrying on parallel labors in his.

Scholarship has, then, a valid and vital place in religion. What about the other side of the shield? Has religion any rightful place in scholarship? Indeed it has: and this is effectively proved even by many of those scholars who don't consider themselves to be religious people at all.

One's religion is his devotion to his own chosen scheme of values. No one is authentically a scholar unless he is devoted, with all his heart and soul and mind, to the values of eager curiosity, of precise examination, of clear thinking and accurate reporting. The shoddy scholar is precisely the irreligious one, for neither true scholarship nor true religion can for a minute tolerate wish-thinking, or careless observing, or the falsifying of records. The quest of the true, the beautiful, and the good has been from the highest antiquity the quest of the religionist and of the scholar alike; and that quest is the most successful when scholar and religionist exist in the same individual.

Beyond this, religion is a matter of faith. At this point we must admit—indeed, we who claim to be religious must openly declare—that much of the ultimate meaning of religion, and all in religion that matters most, do not lend themselves to precise measuring and guaranteed demonstration. We can be scientific indeed about the incidentals, but not about the essentials. We shall need to consider that point in more detail when we come to the specific question of religion and science. Let me but say now that we can not think to prove the existence of God as we can prove that 2 plus 2 equals 4, or that water consists of hydrogen and oxygen in the proportions of two to one. Our faith in God is faith, and not objective knowledge; and we but weaken the religious case when we try to claim for it, not, indeed, too much, but the wrong kind of thing.

At the same time faith itself bears upon the whole enterprise of scholarship in its own scholarly character. There is first of all faith in the value of knowing, and therefore in that of inquiring. That asking and knowing are in themselves worth while never can be proved in anything like mathematical terms. They simply are judged to be worth while, in so far as one by his own faith holds them to have value for him. There is faith also in the meaning of evidence, and in the trustworthiness of our senses as we examine that evidence; and here again we can't prove that our senses give us infallible reports either of sacred documents or of sedimentary deposits. We just assume they do, which is to say we have faith that they do.

Faith in values, which is the very essence of religion, thus is integral to any serious and respectable pursuits of the scholar, in whatever field he may apply his values of concern and his faith in his methods of procedure. That many scholars of today would not admit their own religiousness is true, and it's too bad. These are religious people, all the same, if they are scholars in truth; and so we in religion claim them as our religious associates, even as we demand that they accept us as their scholarly colleagues.

We see, then, that religion on the campus exists and operates in two distinct phases. As a field of study, religion demands of its students complete intellectual integrity, wholly dispassionate and detached observation, absolute willingness to follow the evidence through to whatever conclusion it may require. This may cause emotional strain for some people at the outset; but scarcely more than when young historians first become aware that not all American statesmen have been plaster saints, and not all American policies free from selfish motives. The gain in knowing the facts is greater far than the pain of discarding unjustified notions and inherited prejudices; and nothing worth while in any field ever is lost by our being honest about it.

Many of you, I hope (and I'd like it to be all of you) sooner or later will enrich your formal education by gaining a direct and scholarly acquaintance with religion in its aspect as a formal discipline. The other phase of the relationship between scholarship and religion, however, applies even more widely. All of us, if our college experience is to be of any use to us at all, must be prepared to apply the religious values of curiosity and thoroughness and integrity to whatever study we may be engaged in at any given time. That is to say, we all have the chance to become scholars in religion. This is an elective highly to be esteemed. At the same time, all of us are obligated to be always religious in our scholarship. This is an absolute prerequisite to any meaningful learning.

The beginning of wisdom is the fear of the Lord, expressed in reverent dealing with this His wonderful universe. The religious person will be ready ever to give a reason of the hope that is in him: and that requires reverent inquiry into all the universe too. Here in this College we study religion. Here we try also to be religious in all of our studying. We welcome you, then, to study in religious devotion, and to learn of religion by the method of study. The dual opportunity is yours. If you accept it gladly, you will find it to be to your own great gain.

Religion and the Fine Arts

4 October 1953, at the Holy Communion. I Corinthians
1:4–8; St. Matthew 22:34–46.

* * *

*Thou shalt make holy garments for Aaron thy brother for
glory and for beauty.*—Exodus 28:2.

*Speaking to yourselves in psalms and hymns and spiritual
songs, singing and making melody in your heart to the Lord.*
—Ephesians 5:19.

It is a commonplace that religion is the mother of all the arts.
It would seem, therefore, that in our thought about religion and
the fine arts, we should be discussing the happy affairs of a happy
family. As does occur sometimes within families, however, there
has been in recent years something of a family squabble; and, as
in most family squabbles, there probably is a measure of blame
to be placed on either side. I want to plead again for peace and
understanding, now between religion and art as previously between religion and scholarship.

We do know, and every informed artist agrees, that it was
out of the effort to express religious values that all our art forms
first arose. Painting and statuary represented the gods in idealized
beauty of form. Music was devised to sing their praises. Architecture was dedicated to the providing of worthy dwellings in
which they might be content to live. The dance dramatized at
once man's petitions and his giving of thanks, and the Greek drama
discussed most of all the ways of the gods in their dealings with
men. Two factors, however, tended toward the discounting of

the arts in the Hebrew-Christian tradition; and both of these arose out of oppositions and suspicions between competing and contending groups.

The Jews first, troubled by the survival in their midst of Canaanite religious practices which they held to be idolatry, the worship of physical objects, set up the taboo of the second of the Ten Commandments:

Thou shalt not make unto thee any graven image, or any likeness of any thing that is in heaven above, or that is in the earth beneath, or that is in the water under the earth.

Not always did the Jews themselves obey this prohibition, even in their temples and their synagogues; but, as in time it became firmly established, it did reduce seriously the interest and activity in any graphic or plastic art at all. Music meanwhile was maintained, and was carried to a high point in the temple ritual which was developed after the Babylonian exile.

Then came the early Christians, who were Jewish in orientation and therefore were already conditioned against painting and sculpture. But they soon became anti-Jewish in their attitudes, and so they lost touch also with the religious music that the Jews had created and preserved. The first few Christian generations, moreover, belonged to the less privileged classes in Greco-Roman society, and accordingly had little either of training in artistic expression or of opportunity to engage in it. The New Testament nowhere uses the word "beauty," and few of the first Christians seem to have been at all conscious of beauty as a value in itself.

If we skip now some fourteen centuries, we can see the same process repeating itself in the Protestant Reformation. Actually, the Christian religion in Europe and the Near East soon had begun to make terms with art in all its variety, and the broken family had become gloriously reunited in the Middle Ages. But when the Protestants cut themselves off from Roman authority, they rejected also most of the works and usages of Rome. The great cathedrals remained Roman except in England, the frescoes and images and symbols again were seen as being idolatrous, and the music of the historic Church was discarded along with the Latin texts which it had been created to convey.

Here in America the conditions of colonial and frontier life intensified the separation. Neither the materials nor the skills for artistic achievement were available, even if there had been the interest and the time, which in point of fact were lacking as well. The typical religion of Protestant America became thus a very sparse and literal affair, with its music limited to a folk-song range, its architecture unimaginative and largely unconsidered, its painting almost non-existent and its sculpture absolutely so except for gravestones. The dance and the theater too had fallen under religious condemnation, even as they had in early Christian days. All in all, American religion got along without art; and so it is not surprising that, as art did begin to grow up in America, it very largely got along without religion.

This situation was made the more decisive, and in Europe as well as here, by the negative attitude toward religion of that eighteenth century mood which was known as that of "the Enlightenment." No longer did the painter paint primarily for the Church, nor the musician write principally chants and masses. Painting and sculpture became secular matters, presenting secular subjects and paid for by private patrons. The organ had been a church instrument, but the piano and the symphony orchestra developed outside the Church. The theater from the middle Renaissance on had been pronouncedly non-religious in its themes and its attitudes, and the developing ballet took root where only it could, in this same theatrical soil.

We have not yet escaped from the effect of these conflicts and separations of the past. Art remains dominantly a secular affair, and religion in many of its expressions is almost wholly lacking in artistic sensitivity, appreciation, and achievement. But that something is so does not necessarily mean that it is right; and while today no one proposes that art shall be limited, as it was in medieval times, to specifically churchly purposes only, I do propose that it is time for religion to make much more use of art, and of good art, than it has for the past four hundred years in northern Europe and North America.

The Roman Catholic tradition, of course, never suffered the violent break from artistic interest and practice that marked so much of the Protestant story. The Roman Church retained her cathedrals in all their splendor; she preserved her musical tradition in plainsong and added polyphony to it; she continued to treat her services as sacred dramas of movement and light and color. The Anglicans and Lutherans to a considerable extent avoided the worst Philistinisms of the other Protestants, and now are leading the way in a conscious revival of religious concern with aesthetic values.

And why should not the rest of us follow? Idolatry surely is a smaller danger for us nowadays than is spiritual dullness; and so painting and statuary rightly may be called upon again to awaken the eyes of our spirits. Funereal black is not a fitting expression of Christian gladness in a joyful faith; and so there is no need that the ministers of the Christ, when leading services in his honor, should restrict themselves to black coats or even to black robes. We always have continued to sing, I suppose because we simply couldn't help it; but we may as well learn to sing good music well, instead of poor music badly. The drama, too, can speak of faith as well as of flippancy, and the patterns of the dance once more may represent the purposes of God.

A small Chapel such as ours in the nature of the case can indulge in nothing grandiose or spectacular. But through the years the successive student Chapel Committees have made our place of worship (which once was a clubhouse centering on the side-wall fireplace) increasingly beautiful in line and in color; and I hope you who are oldtimers have noticed the effect of this past summer's raising of the level of our whole sanctuary area. The Chapel's music, too, has improved steadily, alike in selection and in performance, as experiment has created welcome experience and experience has led to new experiment. This morning, as we engage together in the sacred drama of the Holy Communion, we consecrate the visual impact, the musical rejoicing, the kinetic participation, all toward the realizing of the sacrifice of the Christ once made for all eternity, and the sacred fellowship of his people renewed and continued throughout all the generations.

It is beauty that we have about us. It is beauty to which we listen, and which with your own voices you help to create. I pray that there may be beauty also as my fellow ministers and I serve here at the altar in the hope of serving truly you who are his people.

The Fra Angelico reproductions on our walls belong to Florence in the fifteenth century. The cross on our altar is even older in design, and the crucifix above it is a Swiss monastic copy of a very ancient Egyptian monastic model. The music we are using today for the Communion dates from the ninth century to the fifteenth, but its basic style was fixed by Pope Gregory I almost fourteen hundred years ago. Thus the Church seeks to preserve and to use all that is best in its heritage from all the centuries past.

But true art is not only a matter of the right appreciation of the old, healthy and necessary as it may be for us to learn that lesson. Art is still more a matter of vital creation of the new. Not only Palestrina and Bach and Haydn and Mozart, but also Walton and Vaughan Williams, Milhaud and Stravinsky, are musical spokesmen of living religious faith. Not only the medieval mystery plays, but also the works of Dorothy Sayers and T. S. Eliot, dramatize the eternal reliving of the basic patterns of human devotion. Not only the cathedrals of Chartres and Amiens, but also the Matisse Chapel of the Rosary at Vence in France, and Vincent Raney's superbly daring Chapel of St. Ann at Palo

Alto, are buildings dedicated to the present worship of the ever living God.

Elsewhere I have argued at some length that not medieval Gothic, but architecture fully in the contemporary manner, is the right choice for the churches we are building in this twentieth century. It is my profound hope that our new Chapel here on the campus will speak profoundly of its ancient heritage, but that it will declare no less definitely its full and recognized relevance to modern life. And it is my eager hope that not only the building itself, but all of its decoration equally, will represent the artistic creativity of our own artists here at Mills. Some of you, perhaps, will contribute to that end in designing, in carving and weaving and painting; and as you do you will be helping to restore that natural and proper unity of religion with art which so long and so sadly both art and religion have lost.

There are few better ways of serving God than in the creating of objects and sounds of beauty to declare his praise. There is no better way of using beauty than in the expression of the divine glory. I ask you religious people to be aware always of the nature and meaning of art. I ask you artists to be newly aware of the nature and meaning of religion. And I invite all of you now to share in that union of art and religion, of external act and inward experience, which is the Holy Communion of our historic faith. May we find true glory and beauty as we make melody in our hearts unto the Lord.

Religion and the Natural Sciences

11 October 1953. Psalm 19:1–4, 7–9, 14; Job 28; St. Matthew 6:25–33.

* * *

Where shall wisdom be found? and where is the place of understanding? . . . The depth saith, It is not in me: and the sea saith, It is not with me. . . . Behold, the fear of the Lord, that is wisdom; and to depart from evil is understanding.— Job 28:12, 14, 28.

There is a great deal of magnificent nature poetry in the scriptures of the Hebrew people: not only in the book of Psalms, but also in the writings of the prophets, and reaching perhaps its highest peak in this twenty-eighth chapter of the book of Job. We should notice, however, that this ancient Jewish interest in the natural world is specifically poetic and religious, and not at all what we would call scientific. This particular chapter, from which our Old Testament lesson was taken, is philosophical in a sense; but its philosophy of science is simply to the effect that man never can hope to understand the phenomena of this natural world in which he lives, and that he may as well give up trying to.

The Jews of the Old Testament days scarcely are to be blamed because they were not exact scientists. As a people they had plenty of other things to keep them busy: making a living out of the ungenerous and unproductive little country that was their home, struggling to preserve their national identity under the ceaseless pressure of the aggressive military empires that were all around them, trying to maintain their loyalty to a God who made on them the sternest sort of ethical demands. Only in Greece in that ancient Mediterranean world did there arise anything in the nature of real scientific curiosity; and even where the right questions were asked by the inquisitive mind, as in the case of Aristotle, not many of the right answers were found because the necessary tools of inquiry simply weren't available.

No, there is no real problem in the fact that the Bible is short on scientific precision. There is no reasonable ground for expecting that it should have it. Difficulty has arisen only because some people have supposed that it should, and therefore have insisted that it has. This view, the one held by those who are called "fundamentalists," is responsible for most of the supposed conflict between science and religion. The Old Testament writers took for granted a flat and stationary earth, and a separate, special creation of every species of living thing. So did practically everyone else in those times, and for many centuries after; and again there is no problem so long as no one today tries to contend that they were right.

This is our first proposition, then, and an absolutely necessary one to clear the ground for more important matters: the Bible is not, and should not be expected to be, a textbook of science. It is concerned not with the details of the physical processes of life, but with the meaning of life in its furthest outreach and in its ultimate spiritual relationships. "The Holy Scriptures," said St. Augustine early in the fifth century after Christ, "say nothing of the nature of the physical universe, since this is not necessary to man's salvation." How much trouble and confusion we would have been saved if more people both inside and outside the Church had heard and heeded that ancient word of sanity!

But while the natural sciences are not necessary for man's salvation, they are essential to his information; and their by-products in technology, in medicine, and in psychological understanding have done great things for human comfort and happiness. The religious person therefore will not ignore science, will not reject it, will not dispute its methods and its findings in its own scientific realm. "What do you modern theologians think about evolution?" challenged a professor of zoology at a great private university, once church-connected. And he seemed genuinely surprised at the obvious reply: "What we theologians think about evolution, sir, is what you zoologists tell us to think today, until tomorrow you tell us something different."

Actually, although the Jews had no conscious scientific curiosity as such, they availed themselves as a matter of course of whatever knowledge did exist in their world. The earlier of our two accounts of creation in the book of Genesis (that in the second chapter) is a very limited one, assuming the existence of the earth and telling only a beautifully naïve tale of the beginnings of man, plants, and animals—and then of the last and crowning glory, woman. Centuries later the Jewish people came under the political rule and the intellectual influence of Babylon; and when in the fifth century B.C. the Jewish priests retold the story of the origins of all things they did so in terms of a Babylonian universe and of Babylonian ("sexagesimal") mathematics. That is the creation narrative as you will find it in the first chapter of Genesis. The right way to follow the example of these writers of old is not at all to stop where they had to. It is rather for us to learn from Copernicus and Galileo, from Darwin and Einstein, as did they from the astronomers of Babylon.

This is the sensible way in which to approach the long-debated, and much over-debated, problem of evolution. The evolutionary hypothesis is as assured a conclusion as any construct of the human mind can be. It is attested by biology, by embryology, by paleontology, and most recently in the actual development of new species by causing changes in the numbers of chromosomes. (A few of you will remember the thrilling climax of our symposium on evolution, during the centennial celebration two years ago, when Dr. Ledyard Stebbins told of his development of a totally new species of grass in his experimental station at the University of California.) Details of judgment have varied, indeed, and will continue to vary, both from biologist to biologist and from year to year; but no amount of wish-thinking can turn these arguments of scientists, on points of minor detail, into a refuting of the basic proposition that all life is biologically related, and that its most complex forms carry in themselves the clear proof of their inheritance from much simpler ones. Evolution has occurred, is occurring, will occur; and it is not to be religious, but to be willfully stupid, to deny these demonstrated facts.

Perhaps we in the Churches ought to speak more clearly and more emphatically on this point than we have hitherto. The fundamentalists, in their persistent outcries against evolution, seem to have gained the public ear so completely that many people think the fundamentalist position to be the standard Christian one. It is nothing of the sort; but it may be that, in fear of needless conflict on a minor issue, many of those who know better have kept a polite silence and so have managed to give a false impression. Let me say it again, then, and with all the emphasis that I can: The evolutionary hypothesis has been established, and every religious person who is both informed and honest will admit that it has been.

Does this, and do the other findings of science in other fields, do any harm to religion? Not to intelligent, open-minded, vital religion. But they are devastating, of course, to any religion of a frightened, uncritical, superstitious kind.

Years ago, in another college than this, I was trying to advise on an academic program for a girl whose course sequences had been irregular. There was in that (rather old-fashioned) institution a three-unit requirement in Religion, which normally was met in the Freshman year by a course in the Life of Jesus. It turned out, however, that in this particular girl's case the only course in Religion that could be fitted into her schedule was one in the Psychology of Religion. "Oh, no," she said, "I don't want to take that." "Why not?" I asked. "Why, I might lose my religious experience."

I said to her, and I say again now, that any religious experience which can not survive an honest psychological analysis is a religious experience that jolly well ought to be lost, and the sooner the better. In the same way a faith in God that can't recognize evolution as God's technique of creation ought to be destroyed too, for it is faith in a false God, a faith simply contrary to known fact. A genuine religion will fear none of the authentic findings of science, for a genuine religion is eager to find out what is authentic in every area of human life and interest.

Beyond this, a vital religion will concern itself to identify the meaning of scientific discovery and scientific knowledge for the very understanding of religion itself. A God who works by observable natural law is a greater God, and one much more wonderful, than is a God who, as in *The Green Pastures*, now and then "r'ars back an' passes a miracle." Prayer is not less important for us, but more important, as we begin to realize how our sincere praying works in the processes of our own minds and hearts. And so the relationship between a man and his God, which is the very essence of the Hebrew-Christian faith, becomes at once more meaningful and more marvelous as little by little we learn with the scientists to observe, and to describe, how it exists and operates.

So far, then, we have found no proper basis for conflict between religion and science. We have seen that much of the conflict that has occurred has been the fault of those religious people who have confused the two fields, and so have claimed for religion what it is not religion's province to provide. But the fault is not on the religious side only; and having given to science the full respect which is its due, I shall proceed now to record my disrespect—not, indeed, for science, but for some who have presumed to call themselves scientists.

The first and final demand of scientific method is regard for evidence. Much of the evidence with which science has to reckon is positive, and this is the easier sort to deal with. Thus, for example, astronomy has recognized illimitable distances in the universe, and geology almost an illimitable age for the earth, even as biology has worked out the infinitely complex histories and relationships of living organisms. These things have been affirmatively demonstrated, and therefore they are to be regarded as matters of fact.

There is also what we may call negative demonstration: proof that some things aren't so because they can't be. Many of these are simply the opposites of positive data. Thus a spherical earth rules out a flat one; an open universe denies the solid firmament which the Babylonians and Jews supposed to exist in the sky; and evolution disposes of special biological creation. In other cases the argument is less direct but equally convincing. A physical heaven in outer space, for instance, just can't be provided for in a Copernican universe; and once we agree that God doesn't live in a physical heaven we can drop quite painlessly any notion that God has a physical body.

All these are matters of fact: and truth never can be contrary to fact. But negative demonstration is by no means the same thing as no demonstration; and this is where some of the men of science have gone astray. The existence of God, they tell us, can not be proved as can the existence of atoms. So far so good: we agree. But if and when they go on to say that because we can't prove God's existence in scientific, laboratory terms, therefore God does not exist, they have gone too far; and they have become utterly unscientific, because they have asserted a conclusion that can not be guaranteed by the evidence which can be visually observed and mathematically tested.

That God exists is a matter not of scientific knowledge, but absolutely one of religious faith. Proof of God's existence, or any measurable or calculable sort, simply is not available. You and I can not prove God's being, and no more can the atheist disprove it. We who choose to believe in God do so by faith alone; and it is equally by faith alone, for it can not be by demonstration, that the atheist has chosen to disbelieve.

When we examine the matter closely, we shall realize that all the greater values of life—which is the same as saying all the religious values—belong specifically to this area of the unmeasurable and the indemonstrable. The things that are seen are temporal, temporary. The unseen things, the unprovable ones, are just the ones that have eternal meaning. Not only God, and the usefulness of prayer, and any kind of persistence of personal life after death, are thus outside the reach of scientific proving; but so also are all the values that we call moral: love, and honesty, and courage, and good will, and scientific integrity itself. We can not prove that the good life is worth living; but in faith we hold that it is, and in faith we gamble our whole lives on that proposition.

The first reconciliation that needs to be made between science and religion therefore is that each shall identify correctly its own field, and shall cease to trespass on the other's. Religion has no jurisdiction over what is seen through the telescope or the microscope: that belongs to science. Science has no jurisdiction over the vision of faith in God and in moral value: that belongs to religion. As religionists we shall not quarrel with the scientists about evolution or about the internal structure of the atom. As scientists, they have no business telling us what to think about theology or what to do about ethics.

As religionists and as scientists, I say. But there is a second necessary reconciliation, which hinges on the psychological datum that no human being can be either a religionist only or a scientist only. Each of us as an individual has to make terms with both realms; and so, different as they are and distinctly as they must be separated, they affect and are affected by the same people. Each one of us, however primary may be his concern with religion, has to take account of scientific knowledge and of the technological world that science has created for us to live in. No less is every scientist compelled to make his own choices in the realm of faith; and he is an incomplete person, however great may be his learning in his own field, if he has not faced up to those problems of ultimate truth and moral value which belong to the field of religion.

Out of this integration of science and faith in each several individual there comes at last the third and the greatest reconciliation of all, in the united service of science and religion to all the world of men and women. This is a chaotic world that we live in. It always has been chaotic; but today it is perhaps more visibly and more frighteningly so than ever before, by the very fact of the wider range of our information and the nearer pressing upon us of problems that arise anywhere on the face of the earth.

Science is the intellectual orderer which we need for this chaos. Science analyzes the phenomena, and identifies their relationships, and works out reasonable patterns of cause and effect. Thereby it helps us to think more clearly and to plan more wisely. This is true at once of biology and atomic physics on the one hand, and of economics and psychology on the other. Modern man can not be a sensible and efficient member of modern human society without learning what science has to teach him.

But just as science is the intellectual orderer of world chaos, so also is religion the moral orderer: and this certainly is not our lesser need. Science made possible the use of atomic energy, but only ethical insights will determine whether that vast energy shall be used for good or ill, for development or for death. Science made possible radio and television, but only faith in basic moral values can give to these media of communication a sense of common decency, let alone a message of life and hope. Science has told us where man's body came from, but it is only religion that can speak of the destiny of man's spirit. Science has described a world which operates by natural law. It is religion that sees this to be the law of God, and so it is religion alone that will obey this universal law in fullness of reverence.

Religion and the Natural Sciences? Here in the Chapel we welcome you from Life Sciences and the Chemistry building, you physicists and mathematicians and biologists and psychologists. We ask you to abandon nothing you have learned by scientific method, and we want you to teach us all that we can absorb of the mass of exact knowledge that is yours.

At the same time we welcome you also to think with us, and learn with us, and live with us, in that non-physical world which is the world of values, the world of religion. Not in the sea nor in the sky, but in the experience and the decision of the human heart, is ultimate wisdom to be found. There are those of us who hold, by faith, that the fear of the Lord is the first and the final wisdom. We invite you, while you continue to be scientists, to investigate the realm of faith as well; and if then it approves itself to you, to share our faith with us and to enrich it by what you yourselves can give.

Religion and Community Service

St. Luke's Day, 18 October 1953, at a service recognizing the start of the campaign for the World University Service fund. Psalm 9:1–18; Isaiah 58:1–12; St. James 1:16–27.

*   *   *

Thou shalt raise up the foundations of many generations; and thou shalt be called, The repairer of the breach, The restorer of paths to dwell in.—Isaiah 58:12.

Pure religion and undefiled before God and the Father is this, To visit the fatherless and widows in their affliction, and to keep himself unspotted from the world.—St. James 1:27.

The existence in our College of a School of Home and Community Services bears witness to the conviction that education is not only for knowing, but also for being and doing. Perhaps some of you do not know that Mills was a notable pioneer in another area of action, having been one of the very first colleges to give regular academic credit for work in practical art and practical music. Departments of Education and of Home Economics are less of a departure from the general American tradition in higher education; Occupational Therapy is a rapidly expanding field; and courses in Business some years ago became part of the standard university curriculum.

Inevitably there have been some arguments, and we must admit that there still are some fairly serious tensions, between those who have pioneered in these areas which are largely those of method and of specific training, and the people whose devotion is to the liberal arts as traditionally they have been conceived. We who are in the older fields of learning have been troubled sometimes by what we have thought to be too much concern with the "how" at the expense of serious enough attention to the "what"; and you who are in Education, Physical Education, and Home Economics are not unaware that on almost every campus there are those who, themselves belonging to the older aristocracies of the sciences and the humanities, regard you as social climbers and *nouveaux riches*.

In any such situation the right answer is not the extreme one on either side. If and when a "practical" department in a college allows itself to become indifferent and sloppy about exact knowledge of subject matter, it is rightly to be condemned. Equally guilty, however, is a so-called "academic" department if and when it withdraws its people so far into the ivory tower of theory that they become incompetent to live in the world of men and women. At Mills we have three schools which belong clearly to the realm of liberal education as it has been familiarly conceived: those of the Humanities, of the Fine Arts, and of the Natural Sciences. So long as these three remain alive and alert, they will be strengthened rather than hurt by the association with them of the one school whose stress is on the practical training side, that of Home and Community Services; and no one is a Compleat Angler for education at Mills who doesn't cast in all these pools that are so easily open to her fishing.

Where does religion fit into the pattern as thus we have been looking at it? Surely the answer is obvious. The older learning provides, as we have noticed, for the "what," for knowledge in its own right. The newer disciplines are devoted to the "how," to experiment and practice in methods and procedures. What is lacking so far is the "why": the motive that will tie together significantly our knowing and our doing. It is just that "why," that effective motivation for action, which religion provides.

In the two preceding inquiries we have seen that the Jewish

people of Old Testament times had some obvious gaps in their interest and knowledge. They were uninterested and therefore inadequate in natural science, and they were vigorously negative about the graphic arts. This morning, however, we come to one of the areas of the Jewish tradition's greatest strength: that is, the capacity for practical action.

Both our lessons have represented this essentially practical Jewish approach to life. The unidentified author of what became the fifty-eighth chapter of the book of Isaiah, writing possibly at the middle of the fifth century B.C., is contemptuous of those who profess religious devotion without expressing it in social usefulness. More than five hundred years later the epistle of St. James reiterates the theme, calling upon its readers to be "doers of the word, and not hearers only," and defining religion itself as active service to those who stand most in need of personal help.

This sense of social responsibility is rooted deeply in all the ancient Israelite and Jewish prophets. Among the Christian Gospels it is particularly stressed in that of St. Luke, which rightly has been described as "the textbook of the social gospel," and whose author by a happy coincidence we are honoring on this eighteenth day of October. The same emphasis, however, appears unmistakably also in St. Matthew's parable of the sheep and the goats, with its explicit declaration that "Inasmuch as ye have done it unto one of the least of these my brethren, ye have done it unto me." This line of St. Matthew's points up clearly the basis of social concern as the Hebrew-Christian community ever has seen it. That basis is not one of purely humanistic concern for human beings. It is rather one of faith in a God who Himself is concerned about all His children, and who therefore demands of each of them that he shall give himself in loving service to every other. As Christians we do not serve God for man's sake, but rather man for God's sake.

This religious motive, a theological one if you want to call it that, is the one guarantee of the kind of social concern that will maintain a true interest in the entire well-being of every human individual. Without it the social worker becomes professionalized and cold, an efficient mechanism, perhaps, but not a participating friend. Without the love of God, the professed interest of Communism in the underprivileged masses has become a brutal contempt for the helpless person, and a complete indifference to the fulfillment of his personality. Only as we see the person as an end in himself, and not as a means toward something external and generalized, shall we serve each individual fully; and it is the Christian conviction of the love of God for men that thus sees persons as ends rather than means. The vital "why" in social relationships, the creative "why," is the love of God for each one of his children; and that "why" is realized only in those who for God's love give themselves in loving helpfulness to all with whom they come in contact.

Yet once that divine "why" has been accepted as the basis for our action, we must return immediately to the question of the "how." Here, we shall have to admit, neither the Old Testament nor the New teaches us all that we need to know. Social concern is a universal value, and social usefulness is a timeless responsibility within the Hebrew-Christian tradition. Social situations, however, differ radically from generation to generation and from land to land. Social procedures therefore can not be specified at any one time for all times to come, nor in one particular society for all societies everywhere.

Specifically, the Jewish story is one of an over-riding alien tyranny, or rather of a long series of such tyrannies, which allowed to the Jewish people very little control over the total pattern of their national living. The early Christians were even more thoroughly marginal to the dominant Greco-Roman society within which they lived, and so had even less reason to think in terms of any major social reconstruction. In point of fact the early Hebrew prophets had little to offer in the way of social prescription, other than a nostalgic plea for return to the simple justice that used to be; and the later law codes are similar expressions of a longed-for ideal rather than enactments capable of being enforced in fact. Jesus and St. Paul emphasized personal decency and personal good will, but neither of them had anything concrete to say about the basic revision of existing social patterns.

We in America, by God's grace rather than by our own merit, are in a situation that is different indeed. We are not an oppressed people but a dominant one, not a marginal nation but a central. We therefore not only can do more than could the Jews and the first Christians for the total good of man, but also we shall have to do quite other things and in quite different ways. Just here is where we need, and where every college needs, the School of Home and Community Services: to translate the basic human love of our religious heritage into those specific patterns of behavior which in our time will create and preserve the good life for all the people of today and tomorrow.

No, I have not forgotten that it is the School of *Home* and Community Services. I do think that name verges on being tautological, however; for the first and the most important community is precisely that of the family. "Morality," said one of my teachers long ago, "began when the first family came into being." It is in the immediate contacts of this most primary of primary groups that human relationships first are experienced, that moral values first are tested, that life's attitudes are chiefly determined whether for better or for worse.

Even what might seem to be the purely external and technical aspects of Home Economics are important here. It is important for human happiness that we shall be well and tastefully clothed, and also that we shall be well and tastily fed; and so the courses in clothing and in foods have a genuine religious value in themselves. Mills has done well, however, to integrate these technique classes into a total program of family studies, rather than to treat them as separated items in the old "sewing and cooking" category. At this point there emerges one of the new values of our time; for the ideal family of America today is by no means the patriarchal, authoritarian one of Old Testament times, or even of nearer Europe, but rather a democratic family which shares alike in the enjoying of material things and in the making of group decisions.

The Department of Education too has a significance and a point of view which would have been unthinkable in the ancient days. Education used to be the monopoly of a privileged few, and its primary concerns were quite other than those of daily living. We think now rather of educating all of the people, and educating them for all of their life experiences. The motive still is the ancient one of the devoted quest for truth, but the methods belong to a new society of universal opportunity. In the same way we have learned much about how to provide that sound body within which a sound mind shall have a fair chance to operate; and so the concerns of Health, Physical Education, and Recreation have been raised in these days to a level of respect that would have shocked equally the Stoic philosopher Epictetus and the Christian minister John Wesley.

What about business courses, and a Bachelor of Science degree in Business or Personnel Work or Merchandising or Interior Design, whether in a college of liberal arts or in relation to the religious motive? It is not many years since the faculty abolished the Business major, but ere long it decided to reintroduce it in an altered and expanded form. The world's business does need to be carried on, and it needs desperately to be carried on by educated and devoted people.

In my own school days, on the suggestion of a charming coed, I found myself taking a year's course in typing. I lost the girl but I kept the skill. That skill did much to pay my way through college, and later it led to some interesting work in industry. I pray that now it is used validly for the glory of God in the cutting of sermon stencils and in the making of the dummies for our weekly Chapel leaflets. Don't think you're in a drab and grubby field if you're a candidate for a certificate in Secretarial

Studies. You can make your work as a secretary not grubby, but glorious, if you bring into your business community the power of exact knowledge and the still greater power of religious devotion to the common good.

On this particular Sunday we are thinking also of community in still wider terms than these: of our newly recognized world community, and in particular as it is represented in the program of World University Service. Here again our situation is so different from that of the ancient days, and even from that of a few generations ago, that the "how" of our behavior has had to be completely reconsidered and redesigned.

The Jews of old were practically forced into acute nationalism and exclusiveness in their effort to make sure of their own survival. The early Christians were living in the pagan world of the Mediterranean basin, indeed, but they were sharply conscious that they did not belong to that world. In almost the same way an earlier America than ours could think first and foremost of its own identity, and for generations it was able to go its own way with very little reference to its then distant neighbors.

Separations of this sort no longer are possible for anyone. The life of every nation interpenetrates that of every other, and so the life of every individual is affected by what happens to any other individual anywhere. At long last even the Congress of the United States has begun to come alive to these facts, and more often than not decides that it has to vote down those atavistic isolationists who still are trying to live in the America and the world of a hundred years ago.

As citizens you and I are concerned perforce with national policy; and if we are wise twentieth century citizens we shall support always those policies which admit realistically the existence of our "one world" of these mid-century days. As students, and even before all of us have reached the voting age, we have a parallel opportunity and obligation in the project of World

University Service. Free education, honest education, morally responsible education is not available everywhere. Behind the Iron Curtain it is not available at all.

It is the more necessary, therefore, that we shall do all we can to make possible, wherever it can be possible, the kind of education in which we believe and in which we have been privileged to share. If freedom is to survive among men, it must prepare its own leaders from among the world's young people. Not in casual benevolence for the romantically unlucky, but in sober dedication to the future of human freedom, you and I are called to do our share to help in the training of those who will lead and speak for freedom in this next half-century. Unless we make that share a big and vital one, we shall have only ourselves to blame if the forces of cynicism and brutality prevail at last over those of truth and good will.

In every aspect of our life we have to reckon with the what, the why, and the how. When we turn our attention to "Religion and the Humanities," we shall be dealing again specifically with the "what": though you will have noticed that we couldn't avoid it altogether even in this discussion of the training disciplines of the "how." The "how" we do need, and always we shall need, as the connective between our knowledge and our good will: and to the School of Home and Community Services both learning and religion turn for help at this essential point.

There remains the "why"; and that "why" is the everlasting gift of our Hebrew-Christian faith. The fast that our God has chosen is to loose the bands of wickedness, to let the oppressed go free, to deal our bread to the hungry, to bring the poor that are cast out into our own house. Pure religion and undefiled before God and the Father is this, to visit the fatherless and widows in their affliction, and to keep ourselves unspotted from the world of hatred and bigotry.

Learn the what of life, then, in all the courses that put the facts within your reach. Train yourselves in the how, in this particular world that is ours at this particular moment in history. Live evermore by the why, which is the love of God revealed and realized in love to man. Then rightly may each of you be called the repairer of the breach, the restorer of paths to dwell in.

Religion and the Humanities

25 October 1953. Psalm 99:1–3, 6–9; Genesis 9:8–17; Romans 2:1–11.

*   *   *

What is man that thou art mindful of him, and the son of man that thou dost care for him? Yet thou hast made him little less than God, and dost crown him with glory and honor.—Psalm 8:4f. (Revised Standard Version, 1952).

Homo sum: humani nihil a me alienum puto. *I am a man: nothing human do I count alien to me.*—TERENCE (*ca.* 190–159 B.C.), *Heauton Timoroumenos.*

Our first task, and a difficult one, is to try to define "the Humanities." At Mills the departments included in that school are those of English, Foreign Language, History and Government, Philosophy and Religion, and Sociology and Economics. Historically this is a coalescence of two formerly separate schools, one of which was called Language and Literature and the other, Social Institutions. In many colleges and universities the Fine Arts also are included in the Humanities curriculum, and reasonably enough, in view of their expression of human freedom and creativity. A fairly recent book on *The Meaning of the Humanities*, edited by Professor Theodore Greene (then at Princeton, now at Yale), has as its specific chapters treatments of History, Art, Theology, and Literature. This, as you see, overlaps our Mills classification, but is not identical with it.

Behind our modern academic structures there lies the medieval pattern of the *trivium* and the *quadrivium*. The *trivium*, leading to the Bachelor of Arts degree, consisted of grammar, logic, and

43

rhetoric. For the Master's degree the candidate was required to add the *quadrivium* of arithmetic, music, geometry, and astronomy. Our present organization of course has rearranged all this. Grammar and rhetoric have been given to the English and Foreign Language departments, and logic to that of Philosophy, while the whole *quadrivium* is divided between the School of Natural Sciences and that of Fine Arts.

The obvious implications of this story are first that classifications never can be absolute, and second that an exact definition of the Humanities is quite impossible. Shall I be charged with academic imperialism if I say now that everything we study in college really belongs to the Humanities? Yet I must say it: for nothing human is alien to the humanist, and we humans inevitably are part of every department we set up and every course of study we pursue.

The real distinction between humanistic studies and others actually is less in the delimiting of the fields than in the attitude of mind and the way of approach. Since functionally some sort of separation is necessary in the working out of a curriculum, it is easiest to set apart first those subject-matter fields which lend themselves the most readily to precise observation and exact measurement. This is why mathematics and the natural sciences commonly are placed outside the Humanities program, specifically so called. Then the methodological fields, the technique or "how" courses, show also some basic differences in their necessary types of procedure; and so they too usually are grouped by themselves. Let us note, however, that this is no reason why a biologist should not have a thoroughly humanistic approach to science, or a home economist to the life of the family.

What, then, is the humanistic approach? It is that which sees man as a whole being: that which with Terence admits nothing human to be alien to our interest. Since science and mathematics deal with fixed (or apparently fixed) data of the natural universe, they allow relatively little room for the human element. Since the technique courses are directed toward the achieving of specific ends, they too are to a very large extent limited by the nature of established forces and factors. Humanity is seen most clearly in its own right when it is most free to be itself and to act for itself. It follows that the non-exact disciplines, the non-methodological studies, must be regarded as the Humanities par excellence.

Unhappily, the cult of science and the fashion of computation have introduced much that is non-humanistic—much, indeed, that is blatantly inhumane—even into the study of the Humanities as thus identified. Participle counting in dissertations in English; reliance upon mathematics at the expense of psychology in economics; logic chopping without reference to faith in philosophy; the statistical mania that rules some university departments of sociology (no, I do not regard sociology as an exact science); the ritualistic gobbledygook of some of the textbooks in education: all these are examples of the way in which what passes for scientific method has intruded unduly upon the proper study of mankind by man. Certainly I am not pleading that we shall be unscientific. What I am saying is that not everything in human life, and none of the most important things, can be thus precisely measured and weighed and tucked into convenient boxes in the departmental files.

When we inquired into the relation between religion and the natural sciences, we recognized just the same kind of distinction between the objective facts of science and the elusive, imponderable values of religion. This raises inevitably now the question of the relation of religion to the Humanities as a whole. And first of all we'd better try to clear up the matter of one form of Humanism that has had a lot of publicity in our time. That movement, whose best known leader was Professor Irving Babbitt of Harvard University, appeared to some of us to be less an affirmation of interest in man than it was a denial of interest in God. It has had a strong influence in many of the Unitarian

Churches in recent years, and it has won the allegiance of numerous people who had identified religion only with an illiterate fundamentalism, and who therefore would have none of it. A humanist in this sense is a sort of benevolent atheist, usually interested in the solving of social problems and always sure that if man were given the right chance he himself would bring all his problems into ideal solution.

Humanism of this kind, however, is humanistic neither in the historic sense, nor in that of total interest in total human living. Religion is one of the Humanities, not only in the Mills curriculum and in Professor Greene's book, but also in its universal appearance as a phenomenon of human experience and activity. To ignore it, therefore, is arbitrarily to reduce the field of man's interest, and so to deny the basic principle of concern with everything that man has been concerned with.

Beyond this, it is precisely the religious view of life that motivates and makes possible a truly humanistic approach to learning. As I have tried to say about the methodology of social usefulness, so now I would say about integrity in humanistic inquiry, that faith in God is the wellspring of any vital understanding of God's children, and of any useful dealing with them. It is the affirmation of God, not the denial of him, that raises man to the highest level of appreciation, and that offers to him the highest potential of achievement.

Religion, as devotion to value, must involve itself in all the values that man has known and can conceive. These values, however, all are values of freedom. There can be nothing free about the fixed, external data of science. Our freedom in science is just the human freedom to be interested or indifferent, to learn or not to learn, to identify the facts scrupulously or to deceive ourselves and our fellows. Without the human individual there is no meaning in anything. How great are the heavens! How tiny and puny beneath them is man! What, then, is man? Why, man is the astronomer.

Yet man finds himself studying not only the starry heavens above, but also the moral law within: and this is when he becomes a Humanist in fullness of truth. Here it will profit us to look in turn at the several departments in our School of Humanities, and to ask what human and religious values are to be found within them.

For the moment leave grammar aside, essential though it is as a tool, and think of the literary interests of the Department of English. What is literature? It is the written expression of ideas. Its form is important, but its content is essential. There can be no finally significant discussion of literature without discussion of the ideas it was written to convey. Literature speaks out of the mind and heart of the human author, freely and fully; and so it speaks fully and freely to the mind and heart of the reader, for he is human too. Literature thus is one of the great Humanities, if we will see it and use it thus.

But English letters are only a small part of the world's literary wealth, and the English language is far from being the only (or even the best) medium of communication. This is why, hoping stubbornly against hope in our unilingual American culture, Mills still insists that each of her B.A. candidates shall have at least a two-year exposure to at least one foreign language. The labor is hard at the outset, I admit. But the reward is great, in the chance to enter authentically into the life of another people than our own: and not at secondhand merely, through translations which never can breathe the breath of the original. If you would be a true Humanist you may not funk the foreign-language requirement, may not try to dodge it, may not just slide by it with a series of D grades. Nothing human is alien to you; but you will remain alien to much that is human if you are so stubborn as always to operate in English only.

History and Government represent human living on the widest social scale. The past sometimes does seem to lay a dead hand on the present; but I suggest that this is true not with those relatively few people who know and understand History, but just in the case of those many who don't bother to know, and who therefore can not understand the nature of the social forces which condition their own living and thinking. To interpret ourselves and our day aright, we must know whence we and our usages have come. Only thus can we hope to build the new day wisely out of the materials which we have, and which inevitably are those that the past has given us.

Mills is unusual among colleges in that it has a single, completely unified department of Sociology and Economics. On many campuses there are not only two departments in these fields, but also two that war violently with each other. Our peculiar approach here is specifically a humanistic one, in that we can see no legitimate distinction between the social and the economic life of man. Labor Problems commonly is regarded as an Economics course: but how can one understand American labor without knowing, along with wage theory, both general American sociology and the specific sociology of group life and organization? The course in Ethnic Groups is thought of as sociological: but what creates the problems of intergroup relations more positively than does competition for economic advantage? Nothing human is alien to these social and economic inquiries; and so neither of them can be alien to the other.

At this point let me pause to interject that religion may not be considered alien to any of these humanistic fields we have looked at so far. The literature of every land is filled with religious materials, and the surviving literatures of some include little but the religious. History is inexplicable without the recognition of religious forces, whether in the politics and warfare of Europe or in the settlement of the Americas. A study of American politics which does not take account of urban Roman Catholicism and Midwestern Puritanism is wholly unrealistic. The history of economic thought necessarily includes not only the medieval theory of the just price and the Calvinistic blessing upon the profit motive, but also the much more recent pronouncements of the Roman Popes Leo XIII and Pius XI, and those of the National and World Councils of Churches. No groups known to Sociology are more cohesive, and none exert a more decisive social control, than the religious organizations of Christian Church and Jewish synagogue. To think to know any of these Humanities without recognizing the place of religion in them is to be completely blind to the existing facts.

Then there is the question of Religion as one of the humanistic studies in its own right. I have left the Department of Philosophy and Religion to the last, and frankly because I count its subjects to be the supreme Humanities of all. In both philosophy and religion we can be scientific (and because we can be we have to be) about the history of the past. We must try to find out exactly what Plato and Aristotle thought, what St. Augustine and St. Thomas Aquinas meant by what they said, what differentiated the Protestantism of Martin Luther from the Reformed Christianity of John Calvin. We must identify schools of thought with precision, and analyze religious movements in rigorous objectivity. But having laid this historico-scientific groundwork, we have not finished our philosophical and religious job. We are but ready to begin it.

Philosophy is man's quest for the meaning of life, and religion for its values. Again there can be no real separation, because there can be no absolute distinction. Some philosophies, indeed, will leave God out, and others will include him. But both are philosophical in so far as they rest on honest, informed thinking, and both are religious in so far as they issue in a conscious devotion to a chosen scheme of value judgments. You are a philosopher if you think coherently. You are a religious person if you believe vitally. You are a Humanist in so far as you do both to the limit of your powers.

We come thus to the end of this brief academic trail. Next we shall try to inquire, very directly and personally, into the place and nature of religion in our daily living, in our classrooms and our residence halls, on the campus paths and down in the shopping district. Meanwhile let us try to sum up thus far.

Religion depends on science for scientific knowledge, but ventures beyond it in the quest for indemonstrable values. Religion creates art forms, and uses them in gratitude to express the values in which it has faith. Religion is the motive for home and community service, in its conviction that all men and women belong to the family of God. Religion is the queen of all the Humanities, for of them all it cares most about the total being of man.

What is man? Man is a being only a little lower than God. Man is worth studying, and in all his activities as they are reflected in all our academic schools. Man is worth understanding, for in our knowing all men we come best to know ourselves. Man will be studied best, and he will be understood most thoroughly, by those who see God as at once man's eternal ruler and his everlasting friend.

Get into all the schools of learning, then, and learn from them what they have to teach you. And if you take God with you into them, you'll come out with a true and creative understanding of man.

Religion MTWThFS

All Saints' Day, 1 November 1953, at the Holy Communion. Revelation 7:2-4, 9-17; St. Matthew 5:1-12.

*   *   *

Be thou in the fear of the Lord all the day long.—Proverbs 23:17.

To them that are sanctified in Christ Jesus, called to be saints. —I Corinthians 1:2.

Life is so daily.—CARL SANDBURG, *The People, Yes*, 1936.

Do you remember that camp song which began "Today is Monday"? I can't reconstruct all of the text; but I do remember "Wednesday slumgum," and "Friday fi-ish," "Saturday sou-oup," and "Sunday chur-urch." And I'm a little afraid that last reflects the prevailing American classification, not only as to church, but also as to the whole matter of religion. What I have to say is simply that in so far as this is true, so far it's wrong.

The religion-is-for-Sunday-only attitude has a special history of its own in the Hebrew-Christian tradition, and it is a natural enough product of a long sequence of events. First of all the Jewish people, whose calendar was governed by the moon, marked off the four quarters of its monthly cycle into seven-day blocks called "weeks." (The Hebrew word itself, *shabua*, simply means "seven.") The seventh day of each week was set aside as a day of rest from physical labor, no doubt for practical and humanitarian reasons first, though later the usage was associated with the Genesis story of the six days of God's own work in the creation of the world. This Sabbath day then became espe-

51

cially available for worship, and in the synagogues the major services came to be held on Friday evening and Saturday morning.

The first Christians observed the Sabbath because they were Jews; but to this they added meetings of their own special group, usually on the first day of the week, our Sunday, as the day of our Lord's resurrection. As the Christian movement became a distinct and non-Jewish religion, it forgot the Jewish Sabbath and made Sunday its one day specially set apart for worship.

During the first sixteen centuries after Jesus there was no Christian consensus to the effect that any of the minute Jewish regulations about the use of the Sabbath should be applied to the Christian Sunday. Jesus himself seems to have been negative about the practice of rigid Sabbath observance, saying, "The Sabbath was made for man, and not man for the Sabbath." Fifteen hundred years later that great Protestant reformer John Calvin wrote explicitly,

The Lord's day is not observed by us upon the principles of Judaism. . . . Thus vanish all the dreams of false prophets, who in past ages have infected the people with a Jewish notion that . . . the appointment of the seventh day has been abrogated, but . . . the observance of one day in seven yet remains. But this is only changing the day in contempt of the Jews, while they retain the same opinion of the holiness of a day. . . . Those who adhere to it, far exceed the Jews in a gross, carnal, and superstitious observance of the sabbath. . . . The principal thing to be remembered is the general doctrine; that, lest religion decay or languish among us, sacred assemblies ought diligently to be held, and that we ought to use those external means which are adapted to support the worship of God.

It was another half-century afterward that a lesser follower of Calvin, a man whose name by a singular coincidence happened to be Nicholas Bownd, set the pattern of the Scottish and then the Anglo-Saxon and American Sunday by flatly denying Calvin's position, and insisting that every negative restriction of the Sabbath of the Jews properly applied to the Christian Sunday too. This apparent glorifying of Sunday turned out to be negative in its consequences not only in that the day became one of regulated privation rather than of spontaneous joy. It was even more seriously negative in that it implied that religion belonged to this one day only, and not to the other six. Sabbatarianism, thus applied to Sunday, went far to secularize all the rest of the week.

That fitted conveniently enough into the concurrent rise of the gospel of hard work and shrewd financial dealings which was proclaimed by the Puritanism of the seventeenth century. One fulfilled his religious obligation on Sunday, now become a rigorous Sabbath. He was free then to do as he pleased from Monday morning to Saturday night, not only passing by the Church without thinking to enter it for a moment of private devotion, but passing by the Christian religion also as it might apply in his daily relations with his fellows.

Much of this has hung over into our own time. Many a Freshman has said to me, after an early morning Communion, "You know, this is the first time in my life I've ever gone to church on a weekday." What is much more serious is that still, in the community at large, a yawning gulf remains fixed between the Christian values that are declared and assented to on Sunday morning, and the much lower scale of values by which most people actually operate in the factory or office or store.

Yet if the claims and values of religion have any meaning at all, they must have that meaning everywhere and all of the time. One way of symbolizing this, and reminding ourselves of it, is by holding and attending religious services on Monday, Tuesday, Wednesday, Thursday, Friday, and/or Saturday. In the past academic year we had here in this Chapel a total of 173 services, and only seventy of those were on Sundays. (Incidentally, you may be interested in knowing that the aggregate attendance for the year was 6,684; which means an average of something more than ten times for each member of our resident campus community.)

Deliberately we begin each working week with the early Communion on Monday morning, reminding ourselves that God is with us in our everyday duties as well, as truly, as on that weekly day which is particularly consecrated to our worshiping him. We observe also those special days and seasons that the Church has established in memory of crucial events in the life of Jesus, or in honor of the great heroes of the Christian faith. On student initiative we have had now for several years a service every morning during the reading and examination weeks; and many have found it well to begin a hard day of study or of writing with this half-hour in God's presence in his own house.

The opportunity is always yours to share in these planned and overt reminders that every day is the day which the Lord hath made. The very effort to get up for the early service is a renewed and personal commitment to the Christian faith, and the service has been for many of us a means of inspiration and strength. There is special value, too, in sharing the act of devotion with the other fifteen or twenty, or even the other two or three, who are doing the same thing at the same time for the same reason.

It is not only in the Chapel, however, whether on Sunday or on any other day, that we can be and ought to be consciously in the presence of God. Most of you were taught to say your prayers when you were little girls. I shall not embarrass you publicly by asking you to show hands on how many maintain that practice now. I hope I shall embarrass some of you deeply, in your own hearts, as I ask you what sound reason you can advance for having given up the practice of talking with God on your own account.

In this confusing world, and in this crowded college schedule, it is very easy to say there's no time to pray. And it is precisely in confusion and under pressure that we need to pray most of all: that we need to seek a central peace amid the outer agitation, a clarity of mind to see through the muddle, a courage of heart to meet all our recurring crises. Is life a bit rugged at

midterm time, or when finals are approaching? I commend to
you the regular practice of private devotion, every morning as
you face the day's efforts and every evening as you review its
successes and its failures, as one of the most practical of all ways
for meeting life's issues squarely and for coming through them
creatively.

An hour in the Chapel on Sunday morning, half an hour at
Evensong, one or two half-hours here on school days before
breakfast, twenty minutes a day in the quiet of your own room:
this surely is little enough time, out of a whole week, in which
to seek the spiritual resources we need to get through all the
rest we have to do. But that remainder does take the greater
part of our actual time, what with classes and study and campus
activities, and coffee breaks and playtimes and dates. The next
question we have to ask ourselves is whether our religion still
is alive in us as we go about this daily round.

If it isn't, then it just isn't a very real religion for us. Have
we thought consciously, for example, of the irreligiousness of a
snappish temper? Are we aware how un-Christian we are when
we let ourselves become envious or jealous? Have we recognized
the blasphemy toward God that exists in our being contemptuous
of the humblest of our fellows? Have we confessed the disloyalty
to the Christ which stands in our having allowed ourselves to
fall below our best? Have we seen the sin—I do not speak one
whit too harshly—have we seen the sin that is in our yielding
to a lower standard because some influential coterie has made
that lower standard fashionable?

This first day of November is All Saints' Day, when we honor
those who through the ages have shown most conspicuously their
devotion to God in their lives among men. All Saints' Day happens this year to fall on a Sunday; but perhaps it is significant
that usually it doesn't. What makes a saint is not Sunday religion
only, but most of all persistence in religious living in every time
and circumstance. A saint is a person who is regarded as having
achieved a special holiness. You and I too are called to be saints,

to manifest the holiness of God in the conduct of our lives: and that not only by coming to the Chapel at stated times, but by allowing the divine life always to enter and control our own.

> The mount for vision: but below
> The paths of daily duty go;
> And nobler life therein shall own
> The pattern on the mountain shown.

The worship of God in his house is valid in itself, and it is an essential part of a complete and authentic Christianity. It is a positive aid, too, toward our realization of God's presence everywhere and all of the time. But our Christianity requires of us also our own active and enduring commitment, our own unbroken loyalty: our own religion MTWThFS. Keep religion thus in your schedule, and you'll find your whole college program the richer for it.

In the Holy Communion which we are about to celebrate there is one high point at the Consecration of the elements, and another as together we partake of the symbols of the body broken and the blood poured out for us all. But these high points are not to be thought of as solitary mountain peaks, standing in solitary grandeur out from a dull, flat, surrounding terrain. May God grant us the fullness of his inspiration here in these specially sacred moments; and may it be the kind of inspiration that will consecrate, will make sacred, each other moment of our living, wherever we are and whatever our work or our play may be.

This is our Holy Communion, our sacred fellowship. May it be real in this hour. May it continue to be real as on this campus we continue in our fellowship of devotion to God in Christ Jesus, our fellowship of loving service each of us to each other. Religion on the campus has many aspects. Its ultimate fulfillment is in its daily, unbroken, perduring reality in the life of every individual. Life is so daily. May our Christian faith and our Christian living be daily too.

SOME STUDENT PROBLEMS

How Can We Be Christian on Campus?

Meanings and Means of Prayer

Why and How to Read the Bible Today

The Besetting Sin of Mills

The Sophomore Slump

Christian Marriage

The Lazy Liberals

The Arrogant Intellectual

Can We Go It Alone?

How Can We Be Christian on Campus?

Advent Sunday, 29 November 1953. Psalm 97:1f., 9–12; Isaiah 62:1–3, 6–9; I Thessalonians 5:1–11.

* * *

Whosoever will save his life shall lose it; but whosoever shall lose his life for my sake and the gospel's, the same shall save it.—St. Mark 8:35.

> *Teach us to care and not to care*
> *Teach us to sit still*
> *Even among these rocks,*
> *Our peace in His will.*
> —T. S. ELIOT, *Ash Wednesday*, 1930.

This Advent Sunday, marking the beginning of the Church year, is the New Year's Day of the Christian calendar. Normally its teaching theme is the second coming of the Christ; and the meaning of that for us we shall want to notice before the end of this discussion. But thanks to a question from Nikki Tenneson, we are going to set that point now within its proper and larger framework of the whole meaning of Christian faith and life; and at the same time we are going to focus our attention directly upon our own concerns as members of a college community.

This is what I find on Nikki's post card, the first one I received this autumn:

How can the typical teenager or college student be a good Christian? (Implies the connection between drinking, smoking, etc., and Christianity.) What are the *real* values?

59

The first and the third of those items manifestly relate to all that we try to do in this Chapel, to every service and to every sermon. They refer no less to what we are concerned with everywhere we are and every day of our lives. The second, the question of drinking and smoking, is something else again: something restricted as well as restrictive; and how much it has to do with the real values, with essential Christianity, we can discuss first and briefly, and then set it aside in favor of things that matter much more.

Let us begin then with the "drinking, smoking, etc.," and ask with our questioner what connection there is between these habits and being "a good Christian." It is undeniable that, in the American Protestant pattern, there has been understood to be a very important connection indeed. It is also true, though it seems not to be generally known, that the particular approach of American Protestantism is not only particular but also peculiar. It does not mark Judaism, Eastern Orthodoxy, or Roman Catholicism, in at all the same way; nor has it been included, with anything like the same emphasis, in the historic patterns of such Protestant groups as the Lutherans and the Anglicans.

The variation may be illustrated, out of your chaplain's long and miscellaneous experience as an after-dinner speaker for Church groups, by the following formula: At Episcopal and Lutheran dinners people smoke at the tables. At Presbyterian and Congregational dinners some people go outside to smoke between the dinner and the program. At Methodist and Baptist dinners people don't smoke.

But even that is not the whole situation. There are factors both of geography and of time that complicate it further. I never have seen people smoking at a Methodist function in the Midwest or Far West, but I have on the Atlantic Coast. Methodist clergy smoke openly in Great Britain and in the American South, but generally under cover if at all in the American North. Ten years ago the Men's Club in one of the big Presbyterian churches in this city used to take a regular intermission for the benefit of the smokers; but when last I was down there, in the spring of this year, I found that smoking prevailed now at the tables. And within this past fortnight, after I had written the first draft of this paragraph, I found ash trays in abundance at a dinner of a church whose affiliation is Congregational.

Factually, then, the connection between Christianity and such negative rules as these is by no means uniform among groups, among localities, or at separated points in time. This means that historically there is no absolute connection that can be identified, and no fixed rule save as particular groups have made rules for themselves. Nikki rightly goes on to ask, "What are the *real* values?" And it is only in the quest of the real values that any significant answer can be made.

Sobriety is an undeniable value, and drunkenness an evident evil. The Christian then will "stay awake and be sober"; he will not lessen his immediate efficiency by getting drunk; he will not ruin his whole future by becoming an alcoholic. Cleanliness and courtesy are real values: and so the Christian will not willfully be dirty, will not deliberately annoy his associates by contaminating the air that they would rather breathe in its native purity. I think it is fair to say, however, that we could substitute the words "gentleman" or "lady" for "Christian" in both the preceding sentences without reducing their force at all. If it is actually with distinctive Christian values that we are concerned, we shall have to seek for some other formulation.

A friend of mine whose special field of study is American church history (and who himself neither smokes nor drinks) is working on a theory that the taboos which mark the familiar Puritan tradition were rather consciously invented to take the place of other and more difficult moral requirements. Puritanism, as we have noted a number of times, had a definitely economic as well as a theological and a moral aspect. It was the religious expression of the rising business class of western Europe, of individual enterprise challenging the old medieval concept of a static community. Puritanism tended therefore to ignore any question of sinfulness in sharp business practice, to set aside issues of responsibility for the economically unfortunate, to put the individual's gain ahead of the general welfare. I think my friend's explanation is not a total one, for it seems to me to leave some important factors out of account: such as John Wesley's opposition to intoxicants because of the fearful damage he had seen liquor do to the English working class. But it is clear that individualism in general did tend to produce an individual rather than a social code of ethics, and so to look at individual behavior, without direct reference to social results, as the most evident criterion of Christian character.

The real point, however, is that Christianity never is to be regarded as a code of laws, negative or even positive. Christianity is a commitment of the whole life; and that means that rules as such always must be seen by the Christian as being secondary to his main concern. "Love God and do as you will," urged that sensitive but sturdy Christian leader St. Augustine. This is the same view as that of St. Paul, whose advice about the eating of meat offered to idols was to go ahead without asking questions—unless someone else was going to be confused or hurt thereby; and then the love of God compelled him to say, "If meat make my brother to offend, I will not eat meat so long as the world standeth."

We should notice, with reference to St. Paul, that the familiar golden text for Sunday-school temperance lessons, "Touch not; taste not; handle not," actually says just the reverse. What the apostle wrote to his friends at Colossae was,

If ye be dead with Christ from the rudiments of the world, why, as though living in the world, are ye subject to ordinances, Touch not; taste not; handle not; which all are to perish with the using; after the commandments and doctrines of men?

And since today's questioner is a Methodist, she will be interested to know that in 1737 John Wesley wrote thus to a friend:

Do you refuse no pleasure but what is a hindrance to some greater good, or has a tendency to some evil? It is my very rule; and I know no other by which a sincere, reasonable Christian can be guided. In particular, I pursue this rule in eating, which I seldom do without much pleasure.

All the negatives, of course, standing by themselves as negatives, come out at an absolute zero. You say the Christian doesn't drink, doesn't smoke, doesn't swear, doesn't gamble, doesn't go to the theater on Sunday? Neither does a fence post. We can obey all these negatives without even being alive, let alone being Christian.

It is high time for us to turn to the affirmative, to the positive, to what Nikki describes as "the *real* values." What does it mean to be Christian? One answer often made is "to accept the Christian faith"; and frequently that is treated as if it meant "to have the right set of theological opinions." This at least is positive, and so it is better than mere negative restriction. In the limited sense of opinion, however, it is a long way from providing a complete and satisfactory answer. One can not only obey the Puritan negatives, but also assent to all the theology of the Bible and the Church, and not be a Christian at all. Neither negativity nor theoretical opinion is the distinguishing mark of Christianity. The only true mark, as I have suggested before, is personal commitment: specifically commitment to the love of God, and thereby and therein to the salvation that is in Christ Jesus.

Christianity is not rules, though inevitably the Christian will make for himself some rules for his own guidance. Christianity is not belief as such, though the Christian will believe profoundly. Christianity is the accepting of the revelation of God's love as we have found it in Jesus Christ our Saviour; and so Christianity is the total giving of one's self, the giving of one's total self, into the hands of God. "What is the chief end of man?" asked the Shorter Catechism of the seventeenth century Presbyterian divines. And unhesitatingly they replied, "To glorify God, and to enjoy him for ever."

Being a good Christian on campus—being a good Christian anywhere, any time—is at once a more difficult thing, and a much larger thing, than obeying a set of regulations, or assenting intellectually to a set of doctrines, that have been set forth by authority. Christianity indeed will show itself in our behavior and in our thinking; but neither thought nor conduct is where Christianity either begins or ends. These are by-products, and they will vary in detail according to cultural tradition and individual experience. The source and the goal for the Christian are entirely other. The source is God, the goal is God, and the means is our Lord Jesus Christ.

It follows that it is toward God, and not at herself, that the college student (as anyone else) must look if she would learn and live essential Christianity. "Whosoever will save his life shall lose it." The Puritan rules were wrong, perhaps, not so much in being merely negative as they were in being primarily self-centered. The individual quest for individual salvation, which has marked not only "store-front" revivalism but also much of the frame of reference of our "standard" American Churches, is not the authentic Christian concern. "Thy kingdom come, Thy will be done." Only when God stands first for us, and no one else even a close second, shall we be Christian indeed.

How are we, in practical terms, to find God and put him first in our lives? One immediate answer, and a genuinely practical one, is that we ought to be often in God's house, and among God's people. The student who professes to be Christian and doesn't go to church, whether here in the Chapel or somewhere in town, is rejecting Christianity at three crucial points. First, she is denying to God the worship that is his due. Second, she is denying to herself the opportunity to learn more of the Christian faith. Third, she is denying to her Christian fellows the heartening support of her sharing with them in their Christian quest.

If Big Game night made it impossible for anyone to get up on the following Sunday morning, that simply means that this girl saw the game and the post-game party as the real values for her. If a term paper can not be written at any other time than on Sunday at 11:00 A.M., that means that the time wasted previously was to that girl more important, in the manner of its wasting, than was her joining in the praise of God and in the worshiping community's prayers to him. If a picnic takes one away from the Sunday service, then one can only conclude that to that person at that time the picnic matters the more.

Through long years of observation and experience I have come to take a very dim view of the notion that one can worship God as well on the beach or in the mountains as one can in church. In the first place, where but from the Church have we gained the concept of the God whom we say we worship? In the second place (and let's try being really honest about it) is it God we are worshiping, or just ourselves, when we devote our weekends to our own immediate pleasure?

Yet going to church is not enough of answer for us. If conduct and theology are by-products of true Christianity, going to church is in itself largely an instrument toward the Christian goal. Since it is actually in church that we worship God most consciously, his worship in his house is an essential aspect of our Christian duty. But our worship of God, and our faith in God, and our love to God need other and wider expressions too: and they will find them in so far as our love and faith and worship are genuine.

So far as the rules are concerned, we shall keep on being different one from another. Some will continue self-denial as to liquor and cigarettes as necessary to Christian integrity; and I trust that no one who professes to be Christian will hold these people in contempt. Some others will regard smoking and drinking as matters of personal preference, without moral implications so long as they neither damage the individual herself nor hurt anyone else; and I hope that no one who counts herself Christian will be censorious about these her schoolmates. Some will become very sophisticated theologically, through courses in religion and by reading the Bible and other writings of Christian authors. Others, less philosophically minded, will be content with a much more simple type of Christian faith.

Where are we Christians going to be wholly at one? What is it that marks being a Christian as distinct from not being a Christian? The answer yet again is commitment to the love of God. "Love God, and do as you will." But if truly we love God, we shall will to do only what is in accordance with God's purpose for us and for our fellows. And since God's love is bestowed not only on those who love him, but on all men and women because all are his children, our first practical criterion for Christian conduct is that we shall treat all other people as being the children of God.

Immediately this establishes a set of rules that are for the Christian inescapable. We shall not hate anyone, even momentarily; and that is hard going, for original sin is deep in every one of us. Past not hating, we shall actively love; and that means going far out of our way to render service at great cost to our own convenience. We shall not engage in gossip, in sniping, in petty meannesses. Positively again we shall give ourselves in willing usefulness to the whole community, and we shall count it a sacred obligation to fulfill all the duties which the community has laid upon us. (Thus, for example, it is un-Christian to let the residence hall down on any assignment, however trivial, that we may have agreed to carry out.)

Looking now at a wider circle of relationships, we shall see that the Christian student will not be indifferent to the welfare of our whole nation and our whole world. Now in college days is the time, when information is readily available and experienced counselors are in reach, to begin developing an understanding of the structure and operation of our whole human society, and to identify a scale of values for human well-being that will express in political and economic fact the ideals that belong to God's love for all his people. It is un-Christian again, therefore, to fail to read the newspapers, to absent one's self from college assemblies, to ignore one's future responsibilities as a citizen.

The test of relevance to Christianity is always that of the realizing and the fulfilling of God's love. If truly we love God, we shall find for ourselves both the right ways to learn more of God and the right ways to express his love in all our human relationships. The major question that remains is that of how we shall be able to carry through. What is the power that will enable us to be Christian indeed?

And yet once more the answer is the love of God revealed in Jesus Christ. God does not compel us to accept his love: we can reject it if we want to. Jesus Christ is Saviour only for those who are willing to be saved from their sins. Then the will to accept, the active commitment, the positive consecration of all we have and all we are, on our side come first of all. But if truly we will to accept, we shall find that God's own spirit is available to strengthen our living. If actively we commit ourselves to God in Christ Jesus, we shall know that the second coming of the Christ has occurred indeed: that our Lord and Saviour is vitally present in our own hearts. If positively we consecrate ourselves, we shall live in such an enfoldment of the divine love that hate and malice and self-seeking won't be able ever to break in.

God is the answer, and not our self-interest. Whosoever will save his life, for his own sake, doesn't know what the score is. Only he who gives his life freely into the hands of God, for God's sake and not for his own, is rising to his potentiality as God's own child. "Teach us to care and not to care." Far more than fussing about our own Christianity, our own salvation, we need to sit still and give God a chance to make us Christian indeed. Our peace in His will: there is no other peace, and there is no other way.

Is this hard doctrine? It would be so simple if there were absolute rules to settle the matter. It would be so easy if all we had to do to be Christian were to accept a doctrinal scheme. What God asks of us is harder, and yet it is the only possible answer. What God asks of us is that we love him. And if we do love him, we indeed can do as we will; for then we shall not be able to do anything except what God wills.

Meanings and Means of Prayer

The Feast of the Conversion of St. Paul, 25 January 1953. Psalm 66; Jeremiah 32:6–25; Ephesians 6:11–24.

*   *   *

When I had delivered the evidence of the purchase unto Baruch the son of Neriah, I prayed unto the Lord.—Jeremiah 32:16.

No doubt because student problems continue to be much the same from year to year, student sermon questions tend often to repeat themselves. After I had scheduled Peggy Parlour's subject for this morning, I checked back on the record for last year; and I found that on the corresponding Sunday last winter I had preached on the question, "Is Prayer Useful?" This is now the sixth consecutive year in which the theme of prayer has claimed primary discussion in one of the Chapel sermons; and there is no other single topic which you students have brought up nearly so often.

What Peggy has asked for is a discussion of "the meaning of prayer." With that I am putting also some reference to the means that we may use in our praying. What is prayer? How shall we pray? Those are the two closely related questions to which now we address ourselves.

One looks for "meanings" first and most obviously in dictionaries. It may help us at the start to find out what our English, Greek, and Hebrew words for "prayer" suggest by their origins and in their varying uses. Webster's *Unabridged* traces the English "pray" and "prayer," by way of Old French, to the

Latin noun *prex*, "request" (whose plural designates our *Preces* after the Lord's Prayer on Sunday mornings), and the related verb *precor*, "to entreat." The dictionary mentions also, however, a cognate word in Anglo-Saxon, *frignan* or *fricgan*, and one in Sanskrit, *prechati*, both of which mean primarily "to inquire." Thus our one familiar word "to ask" would seem to carry both meanings; but we should remember that "asking" is not only asking *for*, but also inquiring *about*. The relevance of that, in religious history and religious thinking, we shall notice shortly.

The most common word for "prayer" in the Greek New Testament is *proseuche*, and in this form it represents almost exactly what we understand by prayer in general; that is, an address to God, and very commonly in the form of petition for some divine favor or blessing. The root *euche*, however, is the standard Greek word for "vow," and it is used thus from Homer's writings down. *Pros-euche* therefore is literally "a vow toward," and thus involves not only one's requests of God, but also one's pledge of loyalty to him.

In the Hebrew Old Testament the verb "to pray" is *palal*. Here the original force was "to judge," and very often with the implication of judging one's self. The noun for "prayer," a derivative of *palal*, is *tephillah*, which also is used to mean "a song of praise."

Thus our first reply as to meanings is that these three languages unanimously represent prayer as speaking to God, and that in ordinary usage all of them do include in it our asking God to do something for us. But each involves other considerations as well. Asking is seen not only as request to God, but also as inquiry from Him. To pray is at once to make a vow and to fulfill it. Praying requires one's judgment of one's self, and it issues in a song of praise to the Almighty One. Has prayer as petition, as making requests of God for our own benefit, been pushed now into the background? I suspect it has; and I would say rightly so.

The story from the book of Jeremiah, which was this morning's first lesson, seems to me to provide a striking example of the authentic Old Testament view. The little kingdom of Judah, given some eleven years of limited autonomy inside the iron curtain of Babylonian rule, now is about to lose even its feeble imitation of independence. The revolt of the puppet king Zedekiah is doomed to failure, and the armies of Babylon soon will be taking over both the city of Jerusalem and all the surrounding countryside.

Jeremiah, who for forty years has constituted himself a stubborn political minority of one, has seen this doom impending, and he has made no secret of his pessimism about the national future. Now, in the very hour of evident political and military collapse, he gives dramatic proof of his faith in what is yet to come. Disregarding the obvious threat that all Jewish property soon will be seized by the alien conquerors, and so will become valueless to its former legal owners, the prophet buys from his cousin a family farm in their home district of Anathoth. He pays over the money, secures legal entry of the title, and makes sure of the preservation of the record. Then, he says, "When I had delivered the evidence of the purchase unto Baruch the son of Neriah, I prayed unto the Lord."

When Jeremiah had completed his task, when he had done all he could to demonstrate his loyalty and his faith, when he had risked his personal fortune because of what he believed, then he prayed unto the Lord. What does prayer mean? It means coming to God, indeed. But Jeremiah's case suggests that it means coming to God with the gift of our devotion already made apparent and certain in our own living. When we have delivered the evidence: that is the time when we can pray to the Lord with confidence. And until we have delivered the evidence of our faith in our lives, we have little reason to expect of God that he will hear and heed us.

If you will read the Old Testament carefully, and the prayer books of modern Judaism too, you will find that the amount of petition in the prayers of the Jewish people is very small indeed. Praise and devotion, consecration to God's service and submission to his will, occupy far more of the space than do any specific requests. It has been on the whole a late development within Christian circles that has made prayer, in our common assumption, so largely a matter of suggesting to God that he do something for us. The older emphasis, and surely the more noble one, is upon our doing something for God. "When I had delivered the evidence . . . I prayed."

Another striking aspect of prayer in the ancient Hebrew tradition is that which points to the concept of prayer as inquiry. When the ancient patriarchs pray, we do not hear them telling God what he should do to satisfy them. Rather we hear God telling them what he wants them to do. The Lord directs Abraham in his journeys, and Moses in his legislation, and Joshua and Gideon in their military strategy and tactics. He advises Samuel about the political affairs of Israel, and he reveals his will to the later prophets as the centuries pass. All these men pray; but they pray most of all in order to learn.

This day is the Feast of the Conversion of St. Paul. Suppose we see what we can learn about that great apostle's view of prayer, and about his habits in praying. In the earliest letter of his that now we have, the first to the Thessalonians, Paul says, "Rejoice evermore. Pray without ceasing. In every thing give thanks: for this is the will of God in Christ Jesus concerning you." And then he states the content of his own prayer for his friends:

The very God of peace sanctify you wholly; and I pray God your whole spirit and soul and body be preserved blameless unto the coming of our Lord Jesus Christ.

Only a little later, in a second letter to this same Church (the place is the modern Saloniki), the formula is:

We pray always for you, that our God would count you worthy of this calling, and fulfil all the good pleasure of his goodness, and the work of faith with power.

St. Paul asks also for the same kind of prayer on his behalf: "Finally, brethren, pray for us, that the word of God may have free course, and be glorified."

Manifestly St. Paul's view of prayer is essentially that which we have noticed in the Jewish tradition, in which he himself had been brought up. What does one pray for? One prays for blamelessness of life, for worthiness in conduct, for faithfulness in work, for the free course and the glory of the word of God. What is the meaning of prayer? Prayer is the vow of obedience. Prayer is the judging of one's self. Prayer is the quest for light. Prayer is the glorifying of God.

What are we to say, then, about that other side of prayer, the aspect of particular petitions, that so often we have allowed to monopolize the whole? That Jesus seems to have guaranteed that his disciples would get "Yes" answers to their specific requests seems to be suggested by the promise quoted in the Fourth Gospel: "Whatsoever ye shall ask the Father in my name, he will give it you." Ah, but there is a catch here, if you want to call it that. "Whatsoever ye shall ask the Father *in my name* . . ." That is a pretty severe limitation.

What sort of thing are we to ask of the Father in Jesus' name? Shall we dare to ask in the name of Jesus for easy examinations, so that we can loaf through an untroubled Reading Week? Shall we presume to ask, through Jesus Christ our Lord, for a comfortable income by the last will and testament of a conveniently deceased uncle? Shall we get ourselves into stupid jams, and then expect God for Christ's sake to get us out of them? "In the name of Jesus" means "in his spirit." In the spirit of the Christ there is no place for selfish concern and personal advantage; and so for the Christian there may be no praying, not any praying ever, for such things as these.

The writer of the epistle of St. James believes heartily in prayer, but in his breezy practicality he has no illusions about prayer being a kind of super slot machine into which one inserts words, and out of which one immediately draws commodities.

"Ye ask and receive not," sternly he tells his readers, "because ye ask amiss." It is asking amiss when we ask anything that is contrary to the will of God for us; and so we come back yet again to the proposition that praying is designed not to conform God's will to ours, but only to bring our wills into obedience to his.

What other could we ask, if we think of the most agonizing prayer that our Lord himself ever offered? There in the garden of Gethsemane, "in the night in which he was betrayed," Jesus fought out for the final time the temptation to take the easy way. Arrest was upon him, and inevitable death soon thereafter. Might he not yet escape?

And he fell on his face, and prayed, saying, O my Father, if it be possible, let this cup pass from me: nevertheless not as I will, but as thou wilt. . . . He went away again the second time, and prayed, saying, O my Father, if this cup may not pass away from me, except I drink it, thy will be done.

The cup of suffering and tragedy did not pass away. God's will provided for no easy avoidance of the issue. Jesus' prayer, then, was not answered? Oh yes it was. It was answered truly and fully, as every true prayer must be answered, in the acceptance of what God has designed for his children to experience and to do. "Nevertheless not as I will, but as thou wilt." Unless that is implicit in every prayer of ours, we are praying amiss, and we have no right to expect that we shall receive.

Our praying therefore is adoration. It is inquiry. It is self-scrutiny. It is submission. How rightly shall we adore God? How may we inquire of him? How shall we estimate our own selves? How shall we submit ourselves to God's pleasure? What are the specific means of prayer that we may use to gain these ends?

We can pray, and we should pray, both alone and in the fellowship of Christian people. We can pray with the use of words, and we can pray in silence. Let us consider for a moment these varying means of prayer, in the hope that we may learn to use all of them better.

In one sense we always are praying alone if we are praying at all, for prayer is something that happens within the individual spirit. And we have to be alone very much of the time, even when we are in the midst of crowds of other people. "Pray without ceasing," said St. Paul. This is the first requirement. Every moment of every day we ought to submit ourselves to the will of God, every moment we should be alert to discover more of his purpose for us.

At the same time, we are not likely to pray as fully as we ought, unless we take time also to pray when we are doing nothing else. The hubbub of dormitory life, the tightness of schedules, the press of the innumerable things that have to be done before rapidly approaching deadlines, may make the quiet time of prayer seem difficult to find and to protect; but they make its finding and its use even the more necessary. "Come ye apart awhile," said Jesus to those first followers of his. If we are going to live adequately in this our crowded world, and in these our crowded days, we shall need often—we shall need regularly —to go apart a while, and in a consecrated aloneness to seek new strengthening of our purpose and renewed peace in our hearts.

I recommend to you the regular practice of private devotion, not as a sentimental carry-over from your childhood, not as a formal gesture to please your parents, but as a practical necessity in this campus life and in whatever your life may be after you have been graduated. Daniel could not have braved the lions' den had he not kept his windows open toward Jerusalem. We shall not deal effectively with the horrors and the confusions of our modern world unless we have the windows of our spirits open toward God.

There is not only solitude for us, however. There is also fellowship. Praying alone is essential. Praying together is an important help toward praying truly. For one thing, it is physically

and psychologically easier for us to pray when others are praying too, and where they are praying; and so the habit of praying
in our Chapel services supports the habit of praying everywhere
in spirit and in truth. Even more importantly, the awareness that
others share their prayers with us itself provides a strengthening
of our spirits. "Where ten people pray together," said the Rabbi
Yitzchak, "the divine presence is with them." The Gospel speaks
of a smaller number, but it declares no smaller meaning: "When
two or three are gathered together in my name, there am I in the
midst of them."

What words ought we to use when we pray? Let us remember
that the words themselves are not the prayer, but only aids
toward our praying rightly and truly. Whatever words we use,
they must be our own; and so sometimes we shall want to put
our own words together for ourselves.

There is much of value, too, in making use of words that others
have put together, and in making them our own as they may
seem to speak to us and for us. The historic prayers of the Church,
in all their infinite variety, will do much to help us learn what
praying is about, and what it has meant to countless faithful
people through countless Christian generations. We use many
of the ancient prayers in our Chapel services; and in their using
we enter into the fellowship of other millions who with us have
sought the Lord, and who today are seeking him.

I believe you will find it helpful also to read the Prayer Book
on your own account, and other books of prayers that may be
in your reach. What have people sought of God? How have
they approached him? They who have learned God's way for
themselves have much to teach us; and the prayers they have
used will show us something of the way that they have followed.

Yet the words are not the prayer, and our talking to God is
by no means all there is of praying. In our regular services we
have provided (on the initial suggestion of a Chapel Committee
chairman who was a Lutheran) two separated minutes of com-

plete silence, in the hope that for at least these one hundred and twenty seconds each Sunday morning we shall be still enough to hear God speaking to us. If prayer means the learning of God's will, then what we call meditation is integral to prayer. Take time then, in quiet and in peace of mind, to think the thoughts of God. The testimony of those who have tried this is that God will and does speak to them who are willing to listen.

What is the meaning of prayer? Prayer is our means of achieving touch with God. Prayer means praising God for his goodness. It means asking him for his guidance. It means being honest about ourselves in his clear sight. It means offering ourselves for his service. If thus we pray, our prayers surely will be answered in Jesus' name, because they will have been offered in his spirit.

What are the means of prayer? They are solitude and fellowship, they are words and they are silence. Let us use all the means in sincerity, and so we shall learn ever more of the meanings. When we have delivered the evidence, we shall be ready to pray unto the Lord.

Let us pray.

Why and How to Read the
Bible Today

The Second Sunday in Advent, 6 December 1953, at the Holy Communion. Romans 15:4–13; St. Luke 25:21–33.

*   *   *

Holy men of God spake as they were moved by the Holy Ghost.—II St. Peter 1:21.

The holy scriptures, which are able to make thee wise unto salvation through faith which is in Christ Jesus.—II Timothy 3:15.

The historic teaching theme of the Church, on this second Sunday in the Advent season, has been for four centuries that of the meaning and use of the Bible. This emphasis actually belongs to the Church of England, and to those religious groups which have sprung from it, rather than to the older pattern of Christianity as a whole. The Collect designated for this day, with its striking "read, mark, learn, and inwardly digest," was written for the first Prayer Book of Edward VI, published in 1549. This reflects the new interest in the Holy Scriptures that marked the Protestant Reformation in England, and the effort of Archbishop Thomas Cranmer to give to it a place of direct and regular emphasis in the cycle of the Christian calendar.

These four hundred years after Cranmer, thousands of churches and millions of people still are following the usage which he began; and you and I are among them. The English Reformers considered the Bible to be important for Christian people. Do we, as their inheritors, agree with them in this latter day? And if we do, how may we make the importance of the Scriptures really real for ourselves? These questions drive us obviously to the morning's subject as it has been announced, "Why and How to Read the Bible Today." The "why" is the question of importance, and the "how" is that of method.

First, as to "why," I suggest that we need to know the Bible for the sake of our general education, our general civilization in the heritage that is ours. The entire culture of the Western World is rooted deeply in the Jewish and Christian Scriptures, and it is not to be understood apart from them. We all are profoundly and inescapably influenced by what the Biblical writers thought and felt and said; and that is true whether or not we personally know anything about their writings as such. If, however, we accept the tradition without being aware of its nature and of its details, we live in it in a sort of intellectual smog, rather than seeing clearly and breathing deeply.

Even on the strictly intellectual, academic level, a knowledge of the Bible is integral to a real acquaintance with the worlds of European ideas and of English literature. Much of the difficulty that present-day college students experience with William Langland and John Milton, and only in slightly lesser degree with Geoffrey Chaucer and William Shakespeare, is due simply to the fact that they don't know the Biblical points of reference which these authors took for granted. I am reluctant to suggest to any department in the College that it should increase the number of specific courses required for its major: most of them certainly need no encouragement in that direction. I do suspect, however, that our friends on the English staff would find their task much easier if all their students came into English Literature courses armed with some prior knowledge of what the Old and the New Testaments contain.

Beyond the specifically intellectual aspect, there is the no less certain datum that the whole moral code in which we have grown up, and which therefore we have taken for granted as belonging to the very nature of things, stems from the ethics of the Jewish law and from the insights of the Hebrew prophets, including Jesus of Nazareth. If we are to apprehend that code of conduct rightly, and to evaluate it soundly, we need to recognize just how it grew and precisely what it includes. It is not enough for us, as morally responsible beings, merely to accept our inherited standards of behavior in general. What we have to do is rather to examine them in detail, and to weigh their component factors one by one. And this we can not even begin to do till we have learned specifically what the Bible has said to all those whose moral heritage we now have come to share.

The second "why" answer develops from the former one. The reason for the Bible's presenting a significant series of moral judgments is that its writers were facing, and dealing with, everlastingly serious human problems. This is not only why the books of the Bible were written, over a period of something like twelve hundred years. It is even more notably why they were preserved, and copied and recopied, and included in a growing collection. It is why they were bound within one pair of covers, and translated into countless languages, and became of all books the world's best seller.

Do you and I have problems on our hands today? Who ever has had more? Yet they who wrote the Bible had as many, and very much the same ones. What is our responsibility to our fellows? Cain had to face that one, and Jeremiah, and Jesus most of all. What shall we select as our highest values? Amos and Micah dealt with that, and so did Hosea and Daniel, and so did St. James and St. Paul. What shall we do when all has gone wrong for us, and all our dreams have died into dust? Job had to work out an answer here, while he sat on the ash heap; and the second Isaiah in the days of national defeat and exile; and Jesus in the garden of Gethsemane; and the writer of the book of Revelation as he faced the bitter hatred and biting contempt of all the powers that were. What hope may we think to find in a world gone mad? Abraham had to seek out a new country, and Ezekiel a new temple, and the Fourth Gospel a new concept of the life that is eternal.

Are some of the references in that preceding paragraph obscure to you? If they are, this but establishes the point that you ought to know the Bible much better than you do. Whatever the issues, whatever the struggles, whatever the doubts and fears, whatever the prayers and the thanksgivings, men and women of old have known them long ago. As we share in their quest for meanings, we may share also in their discoveries and in their triumphant faith. But we shall not share meaningfully until and unless we know what questions they were asking, and what answers they found to be sufficient for them in their time.

The Bible is not easy reading, however. If we are to know it as we should, whether for our general culture or for our spiritual guidance, we must develop some practical methods that will make its meanings come through effectively to us. Here I want to make three specific suggestions.

The first is that we ought always to read the Bible in terms of full context and argument, rather than just as a quarry for striking single sentences. It has been well said that anyone who uses a text without paying attention to its context is using it as a pretext. The silly classic in this field is the attack on upswept hairdos in the command, "Topknot, come down"; which is derived, of course, from the rather different, "Let him that is on the housetop not come down." And that is very little worse than some partial quoting that has been done in full seriousness and in absolute if pathetic sincerity.

Proof texting is an old device of the Biblically naive and the theologically illiterate, and it never is a profitable enterprise. We always must read Biblical documents as wholes rather than as accidentally spotted sentences. When we do, we shall be able to follow the course of argument, of question and answer, of the posing of a problem and the working out of a solution. Only in this way can we read what actually is in the Scriptures, instead of reading into them what already we think on our own account.

Equally necessary to real understanding is acquaintance with the specific and various historical backgrounds both of the writings and of their writers. Suppose I were to send a copy of this morning's Oakland *Tribune* to my cousins in England. What would they get out of it? They might do reasonably well with the front page, because that deals so largely with world news and with American national politics, both of which they know through their own English papers. They would get much less out of references to the governor of the state and the mayor of this city, and they would be completely bewildered by letters discussing the activities of the County Board of Supervisors. I fear Li'l' Abner wouldn't seem very funny to them, and they might even have some difficulty with Pogo. As for the sports pages . . . well, that's simply a different language.

In just the same way you and I miss the point of much that is in the Bible because we are not familiar with the original settings and assumptions. The ancient writers, like the *Tribune* reporters of today, take for granted a body of knowledge which they and their readers share; and so they never think of spelling out what is for them the obvious. We don't share that knowledge automatically, and until we manage to acquire it the once obvious has become for us the hopelessly obscure. The Old Testament expects its readers to know the long and involved histories of the Israelite and Jewish peoples, and the New Testament postulates the conflict of cultures in the first century Mediterranean world. We need then to know the history before we can understand the analysis, to identify the cultures before we can appreciate the criticism.

Such essential footnotes to the Bible are to be found in many books, and on the campus they are most conveniently available in the standard courses in Biblical literature. But the footnotes do have to be sought before they can be found, whether in books or in classes. I invite you to this further inquiry, and I challenge you to take on the undeniably hard labor that is involved. I believe you'll find the adventure full of fascinating interest in itself, as well as being a means toward a new grasp of essential and enduring values.

Which Bible shall we choose to read? Mostly we use for our lessons here in the Chapel the English translation of 1611, the so-called "King James" version. We do so because the seventeenth century English style is noble in itself, and because it is in close harmony with the language of worship as we have it in our Prayer Book.

There are times, however, when instead of the 1611 rendering we hear a selection from the Revised Standard Version of 1952, or from some other of the modern English translations. We do this when the "King James" Bible is either inaccurate or unclear; and we have to admit that sometimes it is one or the other, or both. For private reading and detailed study, where the value of liturgical fitness yields even more to that of ready and precise understanding, the new versions are even more useful for young people in our day. The Department of Philosophy and Religion rightly has adopted the Revised Standard as the text in the Old Testament course: rightly both because it avoids most of the translation errors of 1611, and because it uses the vocabulary and the sentence structures which most readily convey meaning to us who read and speak the English of the middle twentieth century.

If you have found the Bible hard to read, you owe it to yourself to try the experiment of reading it in your own language; and that you can do with Moffatt or Goodspeed or the Revised Standard, or with any one of a number of other good jobs of translating that have been done in our own time. Once a football captain remarked to me, after he had been pressured into reading

Dr. Moffatt's version of the four Gospels, "If I'd had a Bible like that before, I might have had some use for it." What we want from the Bible is real use: real use for our knowledge, for our thinking, for our inspiration. That real use we can get, if only we'll read it in the immediate realism that belongs to its words, in recognition of the real world out of which it came, in tracing through the real arguments as the really human authors really made them.

Few sermons are any good in themselves. They amount to something only in so far as they are followed out in life. This sermon in particular is useless if you do no more with it than just listen to it, or read a copy of the script afterward. Our subject is not, "Why to hear or read this sermon," but, "Why and how to read the Bible."

The "how" for us is in clear English, in precise historical knowledge, in thoughtful and critical attention. The "why" is in our need to be civilized people, and in our still greater need to be complete and coherent persons. For untold centuries, toward these ends and by these means, countless men and women have found the venture worth the making. If we will make it, we shall find it worth while too.

Let us heed those of old who wrote and spoke as God's own spirit gave them the power of utterance. When we do, we for ourselves shall find the Holy Scriptures able to make us wise unto salvation.

The Besetting Sin of Mills

10 January 1954. Psalm 47:1–9; Ecclesiasticus 2:1–6, 12–18; St. Matthew 21:23–32, 45f.

*   *   *

No man, having put his hand to the plough, and looking back, is fit for the kingdom of God.—St. Luke 9:62.

We have left undone those things which we ought to have done.—Book of Common Prayer, 1552 and after.

The visiting preacher was waiting in the vestry for service time, when one of the ladies of the parish entered. "We're so glad to have you here," she burbled. "And I thought perhaps it would help if I told you something about our church and our people."

His silence gave enough assent to satisfy her. "You know," she said, "there are a lot of elderly and very simple people in this church: people who grew up with the old-time religion, and who are happy in it. I do hope you won't say anything critical and highfalutin, like some of these modernist ministers do, and get them all upset."

"I see, madam. Thank you."

She turned to go, then swung back. "Of course," she added, "we have to remember that there's the College up on the hill, too, and quite a lot of the faculty come to services here. I wouldn't want you to annoy them by being old-fashioned and backwoodsy—we have to appeal to their intelligence, and keep them contented too."

"Yes, madam. Thank you for your help."

The visitor was just digesting these instructions when the door opened again. A portly gentleman introduced himself as one of the Trustees. "It has occurred to me, sir, that you might like a few hints about our situation here before you preach to us."

"You're very kind."

"Hm . . . Well, the fact is that this is pretty much a company town, and the management down at the mill does a great deal to keep our church going. In fact we—I mean they—they cover the deficit at the end of every year. So naturally we—that is, they—they don't care for any of this radical social-gospel stuff in the sermons. We—they, I mean—they would hope that our preachers would confine themselves to giving the people sound personal advice, like to work hard, and be content with their jobs, and so on."

"Yes, I see your point."

But the gentleman paused with his hand on the doorknob for his supplement. "At the same time, we do have to admit that some of the millhands come to church quite faithfully, and that—er—considering their means—they—ah—contribute quite generously to the parish budget. I didn't mean that you should say anything that would seem to attack the workingman; and maybe you shouldn't say anything directly about the labor unions—there are a lot of strong union men among them."

Another pause; then the janitor, with a copy of the morning's service leaflet. The guest preacher exploded. "Look," he said, "I've just been told that I can't say anything either liberal or fundamentalist about religion, and that I mustn't be either radical or conservative about social issues. Will you tell me just what a man is supposed to preach about in this church?"

The janitor scratched his head. "Well," he murmured, "you might preach agin the Mormons. We ain't got none of them."

It is not my custom in general, and it is not my purpose this morning, to preach agin the Mormons, or anybody else we ain't got none of. I'm not interested, for that matter, in preaching against anybody ever. But I do try here to speak of things that concern us as members of the Mills community; and now and then we have to face squarely up to the fact that we are not perfect as persons, and so that we have made our community not quite perfect either.

I've had this sermon in my system for years and years, and I have alluded to its principal subject more than once in this Chapel. A few events of last fall, and subsequent discussions with both students and faculty members, drove me to decide that the time had come when we ought to tackle the problem head on. That problem, as you know by the announcements and the leaflet, is that of "The Besetting Sin of Mills."

All men and women are sinners, and all communities as well. We all have done things we ought not to have done, and have left undone things we ought to have done. But our sins are as various as our miscellaneous individual and group personalities. Some sins that are prevalent in our general society are not at all common here at Mills; and for that we can thank not only God, but also the enlightened conscience of our student and faculty leaders down through the years.

The sin of greed, which so afflicts our Western commercial culture, is singularly absent from this campus. "What's in it for me?" is not a question commonly asked among us. Few here grasp for themselves, and those few commonly become educated soon to a more generous way of living. Genuine good will, a readily helping hand, a happy eagerness to share mark our dealings together; and in this we may take proper comfort and joy.

Nor have we as a college fallen victim yet to the sin which is particularly that of our country in these postwar years: the sin of intolerance. The notable shrines of freedom in these days of suspicion and hysteria are precisely the colleges and the churches; and this Christian College, by the grace of God, still is a place where people think and let think, argue and let argue. There is much, very much, that I love about Mills. But when people ask me why I love it, the first reply that comes to my mind is, "Because it's the freest place I know." Long may we keep our flame of freedom alight here under the eucalyptus.

There is one sin which is all too common in some institutions of learning, and at every level from the grade school to the university. That is the sin of dishonesty, expressed particularly in an established and accepted system of cheating. Here again we may legitimately thank God that we are not as other men and women are. Such terms as "honor code" and "honor system" may be a bit contradictory in themselves; but through the years what Mills has achieved has grown beyond any merely instrumental system or code. We have here an authentic and vital honor spirit; and I know many in other schools who greatly envy us our good fortune in having academic honesty truly fashionable and popular among us.

Those are some of the sins to which rightly we may plead "Not guilty." There are others, however, on which our record is not so clear. Even in this reciting of our relative merits I have come near to committing one sin into which rather often we at Mills are trapped: and that is the serious sin of spiritual pride.

"You can always tell a Mills girl." I think you can. She knows who she is, and what she represents. She is intelligent, polite, well groomed, poised. And very often she's a bit of a snob, and we as a College have our own communal snobbery. We who know Mills can't help loving her; and quite naturally all of us indulge often in rhapsodic praise of a loved one. We need to be careful, however, when this passes into a mere loving of ourselves, when we ourselves become the primary object of our affections and our applause. We're not that good. We're not as much better than others as we claim, or as tacitly we are inclined to assume. Let us be on guard, then, against the insidious temptation of the deadly sin of pride.

Part of the reason for this undoubted and dangerous arrogance of ours stands in a second sin of which many Millsites are guilty: the sin of social blindness. How often the Sophomores in Sociology say, when they are getting to work on their term papers about their home communities, "Why, I never knew that sort of thing existed in my town." How few of you ever have looked about you as you've ridden the bus to San Francisco, or even have seen the people who share the transit system's vagaries of service with you? Here on these 135 acres we have our own right little, tight little world; and all too often we use it as a refuge from the other and very different realities that are all about us.

I am not fond of required courses, and I certainly have no eagerness to teach one. But there are times when I devoutly wish that, whether by means of Sociology 55–56 or some other wise, all of our campus could be brought to see what is before its eyes, to recognize how fabulously privileged we are among the people of our time and our town, to understand in heart as well as mind the problems that may have passed us by, but that rule the lives of so many others. From the sin of our blindness to humanity, too, we should pray for early and full deliverance.

Yet neither arrogance nor blindness is the sin that seems to me our most common, our least controlled, our most deadly. What is the besetting sin of Mills? You caught the point, I think, when you heard the texts. Let me repeat them now, and this time stay with them:

No man, having put his hand to the plough, and looking back, is fit for the kingdom of God.

We have left undone those things which we ought to have done.

What is our besetting sin? I put it to you that it is irresponsibility.

The evidence is everywhere about us, and all of the time. One sample is bothering some of you right now, and bothering still more those who this morning are huddled over their desks instead of being in Chapel. I am thinking of the term papers that were assigned three and a half months ago, but are being written now on coffee and Benzedrine in the space of three and a half hours each. Another case of the same kind, reported to me chiefly by faculty who have eight o'clock classes, is the constitutional inability (so called) of many students to hear their alarms and get to their eight o'clocks: a malady induced, of course, by their having been needlessly up and awake through so many of the normal sleeping hours.

Akin to these are the phenomena of pathetically small attendances at concerts, and of the scanty number of senior gowns that are visible at most college assemblies. Not long ago a very thoughtful alumna said to me, "You know, I resent furiously every lecture, every concert, every chapel service I missed while I was on campus. And the trouble is that I don't have any idea what I did with the time." The trouble manifestly was just this same one of being irresponsible, of failing to estimate values accurately and to express them actively.

The difficulty is not only general. It is also specific. The most appalling thing in all our life here is the way in which people who have accepted particular jobs just don't carry them out; and, even worse, don't exhibit the slightest embarrassment over their failure to do what they have promised. Failure to perform is a standard and universal campus malady, and it has been for as long as I can remember. At least a dozen years ago a great lady, who had served first as College Physician and then as a head resident, said this to me out of her long experience. And I have had repeated confirmation from student officers, club advisers, and members of both the faculty and the residence staff, in every year that I've been here myself.

There is no need that I should pile up a long list of particulars. Every one of you could supply a perfectly horrendous catalogue out of your own contacts and observation. I leave it to you to do that in your own minds, without giving selective and embarrassing publicity to individuals and circumstances that might be too readily identified. It is enough to recognize that our problem throughout the college is that of the far too many people who say, "I go, sir," and go not.

I do have the permission of one of my faculty colleagues to pass on to you, without mentioning any names, what recently he told me about his own experience and the decision which he felt had to grow out of it. He and his wife do a good deal of entertaining. It seemed right to them, when first they came here, to use the chance to help out some of the students who need a little extra money, by employing students rather than professional maids and waiters to help out at their dinners and parties. But they've given up on that, and turned to professionals entirely; and simply because time and again the (various) students who had promised to come just didn't show up, and sent no word of warning or explanation, let alone of apology.

Now it's easy enough to say, and to some extent it is true, that this sort of irresponsibility is something that just marks all adolescents. It is possible also to guess at a cause, in the fact that up to the time of their entering college most students have had all their major decisions made for them by their parents, and that they have had those parents around continuously to check on their doing what they have been supposed to do. That is to say, up to now many responsibilities have been fulfilled because of outside pressure, while now the dependence must be upon an undeveloped inner strength. But to account for the situation is not to excuse it, and it certainly does nothing to improve it.

Precisely what we are supposed to achieve in college is to grow up, to pass from carefree childhood and careless adolescence into the maturity that belongs to the self-directing adult. When still we act like junior-high-schoolers, after we've gone on chronologically six or more years beyond them, we do two kinds of serious damage. One is to the life of our college family, which can operate successfully and happily only through the active, responsible participation of its every member. The other harm is done to ourselves, in that we are blocking the way to our behaving like full adults in the next stage we have to face, the one beyond the college gates and after graduation.

At once for the sake of the college now, and for that of ourselves and our communities in the future, it is high time for us to
confess our failures to do what we have obligated and pledged
ourselves to do; and it is time that, having thus confessed our sin,
we shall exhibit our true repentance by changing our habits
promptly and decisively.

This is the first month of a new calendar year. How wonderful
it will be, you members of the faculty, if there is now made a
general and sober resolution to get all academic work done on
time, and to sleep enough in the night so as to be able to think
in the morning. How glorious it will be, you members of the
student Executive Board, if this year all the girls highly resolve
to carry out their campus jobs efficiently, totally, and with absolute promptness. How much it will mean to every one of us, in
this year and in all the years that are to be, if this year we train
ourselves to do our jobs on time, to fulfill our promises without
fudging or failure, to be depended on with confidence because
we have shown ourselves to be dependable in fact.

I was working on this script just before and just after Christmas
Day; and among my Christmas gifts I received a book of sermons
written by the Reverend Dr. John Preston, and published in
London in the year 1629. Evidently the difficulties I have mentioned are no new thing under the sun, and sermons about them
were preached more than three hundred years ago. On the very
last two pages of Dr. Preston's volume, pages 607 and 608, this
is what I find:

The cause of the missing of the time, is, negligence, when men are
idle, slacke, and indiligent in doing those things that belong to them,
that is the Cause of missing their time. And therefore you have that
Counsel in the words next before the text, since the time is short,
there is but a day for you to worke in. . . . The doing what we have
to doe with all our might, and with all our diligence, is that which
quickens us, and keepes our hearts in a holy preparation to take the
times, and not to over-slippe and over-pass them.

In London in the seventeenth century, and here in the twentieth, the charge and the challenge are the same. The time is short; there is but this day for us to work in. Let us cease to be idle, slack, and indiligent in doing those things that belong to us. Let us do what we have to do with all our might, and with all our diligence. Let us admit, and then let us proceed to conquer in ourselves, our besetting sin of irresponsibility. Thus shall we be quickened for the things that are ours to do. Thus shall we keep our hearts in a holy preparation to take the times. Thus shall we cease to overslip and overpass the doing of the things that belong to us.

Dear ones, I have scolded you today because I love you always. I have scolded our community because I belong to it, and share its failings as I do its delights. In our love for one another, and for our College, there is ground for faith that together we may grow enough so that we shall need to scold ourselves a little less. In God's love for us there is at once the command and the power that we shall not leave undone those things which we ought to be doing.

The Sophomore Slump

21 February 1954. Psalm 43; Ecclesiastes 1:1–10, 13f; Romans 7:14–25.

*   *   *

Why art thou cast down, O my soul? and why art thou disquieted within me?—Psalm 43:5.

Vanity of vanities, saith the Preacher. . . . All is vanity and vexation of spirit.—Ecclesiastes 1:2, 14.

Miserable wretch that I am! Who will rescue me from this body of death?—Romans 7:24 (James Moffatt, 1913).

Those texts, one each from this morning's Psalm and from the two lessons, are the obvious ones for a sermon about the Sophomore slump. There is another relevant text, however, which well might be taken from the first lesson. That is the ninth verse of this pessimistic opening chapter of Ecclesiastes:

The thing that hath been, it is that which shall be; and that which is done is that which shall be done: and there is no new thing under the sun.

Believe me, the Sophomore slump is no new thing. It has happened year after year as far back as I can remember; and I expect that, no matter how many sermons may be preached about it, something of the sort will occur as long as boys and girls grow up and become young people in college.

The worst spot usually is in the early part of the second semester. Taking counsel many weeks ago with student leaders, I found

94

myself supported in my hunch that this third week in February would be a fitting time in which to discuss our annual failure of morale. Scarcely had I scheduled the sermon for this particular day, when there came a postcard from Connie Boileau. Connie is a Junior; and I have a notion that it was her memory of experiences of a year ago that made her write me thus: "Would it be possible to write a sermon on despondency not being good for the mind or soul, and what can be done about it?"

The Sophomore slump, as I have seen it, is made up of about equal parts of despondency and griping: griping about the College and all its works, despondency about one's own life, present and future. It shows itself in apathy toward classes, in petty bickerings in the halls, in complaints about the food, in bull sessions about "How many people are going to transfer out?" and "What's the use of being here anyway?" Most of this is not good for the mind or soul. We ought to do something about it if we can. And so Connie's question fits exactly the problem as it rises year after year, and as year after year we have to admit its existence.

What brings on this annual epidemic of pessimism? First of all, pessimism is endemic in human nature. Life is made up of all sorts of experiences. The hours that are all fun and joy are few and far between. For most of our pleasures we find we have to pay a price, either in hard work for their gaining, or in weariness when they're ended, and often in both. People, we are convinced, let us down again and again; and only in the rosy and temporary mist of romantic love do we really believe in the perfection of any human being whom we know.

The gentle old cynic who wrote the book of Ecclesiastes was but speaking honestly what all men think and feel much of the time. "Vanity of vanities . . ." Emptiness of emptiness, all is emptiness. "All the rivers run into the sea, yet the sea is not full." Souls are cast down and disquieted everywhere, and have been since man first achieved an emotional reaction to his hard and often fruitless quest for food. As members of the human family, we live in an imperfect set of surroundings both material and social; and as creatures with highly complex nervous systems we react sensitively and negatively to whatever we find negative, or consider negative, in our environment.

You're not alone, you Sophomores, in your singing of the low-down blues. Every man and woman sings them, has sung them, will sing them. And every one who feels blue always is persuaded that there is abundant reason.

But you belong not only to the general category of *Homo sapiens=Homo despondens*. You belong also to the specific classification of the Sophomore. That word itself long ago was applied to second-year students in the universities, no doubt first by their elders, because it seemed to describe the condition they were in. "Sophomore" is *sophos-moros* (wise-foolish); and the Sophomore thus by definition is half wise and half a fool.

The learning process has begun, and the student knows much more than he or she did in the innocent years of childhood. The learning process is far from complete, however. There remain many hangovers of infantile behavior; there persist many childish notions; and there are many surviving bits of adolescent feeling. Knowing so much that is new to her, the Sophomore is not yet wise enough to know that she never will know everything. It is characteristic, indeed, that she seems to assume she knows everything already.

Therefore when common human negativity sets in, it is especially likely to express itself in the Sophomore by a hypercritical estimate of everything around her. She has discovered that some of the things she had been told in her childhood, and used to believe, simply weren't so. Naturally enough, then, from her point of view, everything she has been told in the past, or now is being told, comes under grave suspicion. She has found out that authorities are not infallible. It is a simple next step to conclude that all authorities are all wrong.

All of us here have been Sophomores, except you Freshmen; and you're headed straight for just this sort of thing a year hence. All of us are Sophomores perennially, in greater or smaller degree. Our wisdom is imperfect; and therefore all too commonly we confuse it with our foolishness, so that silliness masquerades as profundity and the ignoramus counts himself a know-it-all. Not only at Mills, but everywhere, there seems to be the highest incidence of this malady when wisdom has not had time enough to become fully wise.

A third factor, and one that affects every one of us, is the college situation. We live in a crowded, hyperactive, necessarily organized and disciplined community. Each of our residence halls has a hundred or more girls in it, and its ways can not be adjusted to the special preferences and the shifting moods of every individual member. The food service operates under the same difficulty, aimed perforce at an average taste and therefore not exactly satisfying any single one of the eaters. Community living at once makes noise and must forbid it, at once creates tensions and has to set up rules to control them.

This is true of every residence college, and of all group living. Mills has a further special problem, and the one of which most of you are the most aware: that is, that this is a community whose basic membership consists entirely of women. I personally happen to like women, no doubt better than most women do; and so I am not qualified to see this particular problem of yours with your hardened and cynical eyes. But I believe it is a problem for you, because you are continually telling me it is. And when the pressure of having too many women around all the time becomes just too much for you to bear—well, then it's ho for coeducation.

The Sophomore slump occurs because Sophomores are human. It occurs because they're young. It occurs because they're in college, and at Mills partly because they're in a women's college.

A fourth point is that the slump occurs in February because it's February. The weather unquestionably has something to do with this, and the slump is noticeably the worse in those years when we have a lot of late winter rain. Even a more definite cause, and a more regular one, is the lack of high festivals in the late winter season. It's a long time since Christmas, and a long way yet to Easter; and neither St. Valentine's Day nor St. Patrick's quite measures up as a day of days. Basketball is no substitute for football as a Saturday outlet; the big ski trip is in the past; and the baseball fans still have weeks to wait before they can begin following the fortunes of the Dodgers and the Oaks.

There is also the insoluble problem posed by the structure of the academic year. We're on campus something less than three months before Christmas, but fully five months after it. With this year's late Easter Day, we have still seven unbroken weeks of class work looming ahead before our ten-day break. The novelty of new courses has faded, and the joy of seeing old friends has become commonplace. It's just a long, weary grind, as far ahead as our limited vision can see. We don't want to grind or be ground, and so the grinding issues in the grounding of our spirits.

This is the way it is, and why it is, and has been since memory runneth not to the contrary. Human beings get low. Young human beings get confused. College students get harried. None of us is happy with monotony. The Sophomore slump is real, and it is understandable. Yet clearly despondency is not "good for the mind or soul," and we needs must ask, "What can be done about it?" What can be?

The quest for the cure demands that we reexamine the causes. What about the seasonal factor, first? The obvious reply here is that it is seasonal. It's just a month now to the official beginning of spring. Four weeks from today it will be only nineteen days to the spring vacation, and but twenty-eight to the Easter parade. From then on the College year will be so full of new excitements, academic and social, that we'll have little time left for worrying about ourselves and our fluctuating temperaments.

Take courage, then. Time is a wonderful healer of all sorts of ills, and particularly of those ills that grow out of impatience.

> The vision has its own appointed hour,
> it is ripening, it will flower;
> if it be long, then wait,
> for it is sure, and it will not be late.

Thus Dr. Moffatt translates the divine reply to an impatient, harried, complaining soul of many centuries ago, the Jewish prophet Habakkuk. It's a long grind now, but the vision has its own appointed hour. And you'll find out when you're Seniors, even though you can't believe it as Sophomores, that the day will come when you'll decide that the long grind on campus was all too short.

The reply as to the College is to my mind just as decisive as that in the case of the season, but it is less obvious and therefore it requires more discussion. Instead of arguing at length, however, I shall report two sample cases in point, and comment on them only briefly. Neither of them, I may say, comes directly from this campus. One specimen relates to the general stresses of community living, and the other to the specific issue of the pattern of the women's college versus that of coeducation.

Case Number One: In a summer school which I directed for a number of years, the food gripe was particularly widespread and vociferous in the summer of 1937. The student council decided matters might be improved if they installed a suggestion box outside the dining-room door. They did so; and from that time on they got exactly two written suggestions. One was that the food was inadequately seasoned. The other was that it had too much salt in it.

You see the point. Any sort of collectivism, even when it

operates under an agency of free enterprise, means compromise of everybody's individual predilections. We have to be quiet for other people's sake, even when we feel like being noisy; and we have to endure a good deal of other people's noise when we most want to be quiet. We have to settle for coffee at breakfast and tea at lunch, though we might want them reversed, because to run a college like a top-row hotel would require charging top-row hotel prices. We have to put up with a miscellany of teachers whom we didn't choose (and sometimes are sure we certainly wouldn't have chosen) unless we are in a position to secure private tutors of our own selection in every field of knowledge.

Check your gripes, then, by asking just what practicable procedure you would recommend to replace what you object to. If your suggestion is really a practical one, and if it is acceptable to the majority, your gripe may turn out to be a positive contribution to the common good. If it isn't practical, or if it represents only a small segment of campus opinion, you're going to have to get along with the *status quo*, and you may as well stop your sputtering about it.

Case Number Two: The Dean of Students at a state college was telling me how much of his time he had to devote to personal counseling. I asked him what was the most common type of personal problem he encountered. "Oh," he replied, "that's easy to say. It's these pathetic little girls who can't get dates."

"Sir," I inquired, "what is the sex ratio in your institution?"

"Nineteen hundred men and nine hundred women."

A few of you have heard me tell that before. I think I ought to tell it at least every two years, to be sure that each Sophomore gets a chance to hear it. The moral is evident. It is that little girls who can't get dates don't get dates, and that coeducation makes not the slightest bit of difference. Within the month I've heard both Stanford and University of California girls complaining about the way you Millsites snag their men out from under their noses; and it is an ancient and meaningful legend that the first bridge across San Francisco Bay was built to make it easier for Stanford men to get to Mills. My own daughter, too, who was at one coeducational college for four years as an undergraduate and then for three years more on the staff, has told me that the annual slump there is just as regular and just as deep as ever it is in our situation.

Coeducation alone scarcely will solve the social problem, and a change of scenery seldom relieves the stresses that have developed within one's own personality. Maybe there are some of you who ought to transfer out. But if you do, let it be for reasons, and not from mere contagion rationalized while you're in the dumps. Things weren't necessarily better in "the good old days" than they are now, and they aren't necessarily better some other place than they are here. Do your thinking now, well in advance; and be sure you don't burn your bridge until you're quite certain you don't want to cross it again.

This brings us directly to the problem that inheres in being a Sophomore. There is a comparable word, happily less familiar, with a much less favorable connotation. It is "morosoph." It puts, you see, the foolishness first; and it is defined as meaning "a wise fool." Some Sophomores are morosophs in truth: emotional adolescents posing as worldly-wise sophisticates, half trained minds assuming their superiority to all their teachers, immature citizens sure that they alone know how to remake the world.

"The wisest know that they know nothing," declared the ancient sage. Certainly the wise know that their knowledge is small indeed; and if the *Soph* part of the Sophomore, the wise part, is to grow, it will have to do so by cramping into ever smaller proportions the foolishness of supposing that one knows it all. Here again time is of the essence, and we your elders have learned not to expect too much of you too soon. But we don't expect too little, either, and the world will not accept too little. You're past the middle of your Sophomore year right now. May you demonstrate that by being well past the middle of your journey out of foolishness into wisdom.

Yet we all are Sophomores, because we all are human. The specific Sophomore problem remains the universal human problem. Despondency is not "good for the mind or soul," and despondency still recurs in every one of us. Again we ask ourselves, "What can be done about it?"

Some of the answers we have seen already. Time is a great solvent, and as we grow older we shall realize that increasingly. Honest facing of the facts of our human living will help us to change what should be changed, to endure what can't be changed, and to have sense enough to know which is which. Honest facing of ourselves will enable us to sort out our real thinking from our prejudices, and essential wisdom from occasional and irresponsible notions. Thus the season, and the College, and even the Sophomore year, can be for all of us much more tolerable than some of us have let them be.

So far this has been, in subject matter and treatment, more like an assembly speech than a sermon. I'm turning it into a sermon now, and not so much because I'm expected to preach sermons in the Chapel as because I'm convinced that religion is necessary to any adequate living. What finally can we do about despondency, griping, despair, self-pity? We can find a faith, and we can live by it.

Religion is faith in ultimate values. It is the full commitment of ourselves to the best values we have found, and to the finding and realizing of the best that yet we may discover. Social realism, and honesty with ourselves, are among the values, and they are useful as instruments; but they are not all we need for the growing of a confident and competent human spirit.

Only as we search for those values that have absolute meaning in the framework of eternity can we hope to deal adequately with the immediate difficulties of the passing moment. Only as we catch a clear vision of the greater things shall we see the petty ones in their true and insignificant proportions. Only as we gamble our lives on doing the will of God as we conceive it, can we hope that God will justify our faith by giving us the grace to endure the testing that has to be ours.

Oh, yes, we shall slump again, because we're human. And we shall rise again, human though we are, if we lay hold on the resources that are divine, and are within our reach. There is a place for us to fill in life, and we can fill it. We can fill it if by our own complete commitment of ourselves we make available to us the grace of God himself.

Despondency is not good for mind or soul. Griping destroys much more of good than ever it does of ill. The Sophomore slump is a costly waste of time and mental power and spiritual force. February is near its end, and the slump should be too. It can be.

Why art thou cast down, O my soul? and why art thou disquieted within me? Hope thou in God, for I shall yet praise him, who is the help of my countenance, and my God. Miserable wretch that I am! Who will rescue me from this body of death? God will! Thanks be to him through Jesus Christ our Lord.

The Sophomore slump? For God's sake, and for your own, snap out of it.

Christian Marriage

16 January 1955. Psalm 128; Proverbs 31:10–31; St. Mark 10:6–16.

✻ ✻ ✻

The Lord God said, It is not good that the man should be alone.—Genesis 2:18.

From the beginning of the creation God made them male and female. For this cause shall a man leave his father and mother, and cleave to his wife; and they twain shall be one flesh.—St. Mark 10:6–8.

On the first Sunday of last December we thought together of Maeva Hair's question about the nature of prayer. Her post card of the early autumn mentioned another subject also, the one to which we turn today. It is that of "Christian marriage."

Only ten months ago, as some of you may remember, our subject here was "Marriage Ancient and Modern." That morning we examined, on the basis of a series of questions from Mr. Winthrop Keep, a good deal of historical material about marriage customs and regulations in the Old Testament world, in early Christian times, in the Middle Ages and the Renaissance, and in our culture of today. I shan't repeat in those areas this time, except when reference to them may serve as illustration. Instead I shall attempt what I assume Mev wants: an inquiry into the basic Christian positions about marriage, the essential Christian ideals of married life.

First let us think about the prelude to marriage, in Christian courtship. Then I shall seize the chance to say a few words about a matter which I think is more important than is generally recognized: the nature and meaning of a Christian wedding. Finally, and at a little greater length, we'll ask ourselves about the character of a truly Christian household.

Courtship in this country in our time is manifestly a much freer enterprise and experience than it has been in most societies in most of human history. The freedom of individual choice, though it is restricted to some extent by circumstance, is technically absolute for those who have reached the age the law regards as adult. Parents do not have their former authority over their sons and daughters; the bride-price and the dowry survive only in the symbolism of wedding gifts; and the marriage broker is to our minds an unbelievable curiosity.

The yellow-backed novel of Victorian romanticism, and the corresponding products of Hollywood in this century, seem to have established "Love laughs at locksmiths" as an article of universal and unquestioned faith. The old barriers of ancestry, class, education, and religion have been broken down so often that many no longer think of them as existing; and in recent years, though to a smaller extent, differences of nationality and what is called "race" have been challenged as being no proper bar to the setting up of a new family.

New freedoms, however, always carry with them new problems and new responsibilities. We as Americans are committed to freedom, in this area as in so many others. We as Christians therefore ought soberly to consider what this freedom of individual choice demands of us in terms of intelligent and constructive decision.

I believe you will agree that Christian marriage, in fundamental principle, looks toward stable human relationships rather than merely toward exciting adventures. The old order, with its narrower limits of selection, brought together men and women who had similar backgrounds, who thought in similar terms, who held much the same value-judgments. This made for relative ease of adjustment between the marriage partners, and so for stability in the carrying forward of an already familiar pattern of life. The tradition of romantic love, on the other hand, has encouraged attempts to set up households where many values are not shared, where interests vary and often clash, where outside pressures work in contrary directions.

The settling down together of a man and a woman—of any man and any woman—is a subtle and difficult process at best. Any point of difference between the two is an added point of potential danger. The case of marriage across religious lines provides a striking example. A recent study of six thousand marriages showed these figures: where both sets of parents were Protestant, 6.8 per cent ended in separations; where both were Roman Catholic, 6.4 per cent; but where one was Protestant and one Roman Catholic, the ratio of separations was 15.2 per cent, almost two and one half times as great. (It is worth noting that in those cases where there was no religious affiliation at all, the rate was even higher, being 16.7 per cent.)

This is not to say a mixed marriage can't possibly work; but it does indicate that its chances of survival are not nearly so good as in the case of a couple who hold a common faith. And when one adds to this the high probability that an apparently successful marriage of this sort will have become so by making the compromise of dropping both religious loyalties, one wonders what the percentage is of such marriages that rightly may be described as Christian.

At the risk of assailing all the dearly held superstitions that the movies have fostered, I put it to you that falling in love is not an inevitable act of the inscrutable God, but principally a voluntary act on the part of the human being. The choice of a marriage partner is not sufficiently validated by an evening of ecstasy at the spring formal, and it is not authenticated by an eager curiosity about a way of living and thinking that fascinates just because it seems exotic. The more nearly a man and woman have shared experiences up to the time of their wedding, the more likely they are to share happily in their life together afterward.

This carries the corollary that a reasonable time of personal acquaintance before marriage is also a safeguard and a help. Several years ago a Senior in one of my classes offered the interesting proposal that the issuance of a marriage license should be conditioned on a waiting period of one year from the first filing, and the payment of a fee of at least $500. "Then," she said, "we might be able to afford to grant divorces for two dollars on request." You see her point: a primary cause of marriage failure is hasty and thoughtless selection at the outset. Christian judgment never is permitted to be thoughtless or hasty; and so Christian courtship will be sane, considered, and constructive. Scarcely otherwise may we expect Christian marriage to occur.

Now a word about weddings. A wedding has three aspects. It is a happy social occasion. It is a production. And it is a religious consecration. Unless it is this last, it is not a Christian ceremony, and it makes no contribution to a Christian marriage.

The production factor can be a useful servant of the religious purpose, if it is regarded and treated thus. But if instead its emphasis is on the social side at the expense of the religious, it has no place in the house of God. A good deal of my time in marriage conferences is devoted to trying to cut down needless and expensive display, in the interests at once of seriousness, of good taste, and of financial saving for the sake of the household that is being established.

A few flowers in the sanctuary, tastefully arranged, are beautiful and satisfying. A massive display is vulgar. A few near friends of bride and groom well may have a part in the service. An army of bridesmaids and ushers, invited in order to satisfy supposed social obligations, is a burden not only upon the minister but also upon the couple and upon both sets of parents. A little quiet organ music, and a dignified march tune, will help to create a relaxed and cheerful mood. A tremolo warbling of musical comedy love songs is an affront to the seriousness of a Christian ceremony, and the banalities of the *Lohengrin* "Bridal Chorus" belong only to the decadent period of opera from which they came.

I speak as a veteran of these campaigns, and as one who bears many scars from pre-wedding skirmishes. The typical "big wedding" is economically an outrageous waste of money, and spiritually it is a denial of the intensely solemn and personal matters which are involved. I fear it is true that often it is the bride's mother, rather than the bride herself, who wants the occasion to be a splurge. If by any chance your mothers try to force anything of the sort on you, I hope you will stand your ground for dignity and simplicity. It's your marriage, not hers; and if you are Christian you will want a Christian and not a pagan ceremony.

O.K. The vows have been said; the cake has been cut; you've had a glorious week at Carmel. Now comes the time of testing: the lifetime of testing. The continuingly close quarters of a household are very different from the occasional holding of hands in the little living room in Orchard-Meadow Hall. The problems of getting breakfast every morning are tougher than those of reading the Friday evening menu at the Sea Wolf. The paying of the installments on the house and the car comes harder than the buying of a corsage for you or a Christmas necktie for him. The strains of routine are greater far than the stresses of excitement. Are you going to be equal to them?

The Christian couple will be, if they are Christian. Here we need to consider carefully the character of Christian love. Not infatuation, but good will, is the key to the secret; not passionate possessing, but patient consideration; not satisfaction for one's self, but concern to serve the loved one. We need to ask ourselves always whether it is the other person we are loving, or just ourselves.

A great deal of what commonly is called "love" is nothing but self-seeking and self-gratification. If both members of a marriage care for themselves primarily, the chances of their building a happy home are slight. If one of them genuinely gives love, and the other only takes, the marriage may survive; but it is scarcely worthy to be called Christian. Only if each of them loves the other for that other's sake, and not for his or her own, will a truly Christian unity and fulfillment be possible.

It took me some time, on the morning after Thanksgiving Day, to decide on the lessons and the texts for this service. I thought first of the lilting and soaring love songs that are put together in the book called "The Song of Songs" (which of course is not Solomon's, but is of much more recent date). I was much attracted by such a line as, "Set me as a seal upon thine heart, as a seal upon thine arm." But then I read the rest of the verse:

For love is strong as death; jealousy is cruel as the grave: the coals thereof are coals of fire, which hath a most vehement flame.

It's too true. The love that would consume the loved one in the fire of possessiveness is deadly indeed, and the jealousy that springs from it becomes a cruelty that is altogether un-Christian. The Song of Songs is romanticism almost wholly unrestrained; and if, as is thought by many scholars, it is a collection of songs sung at wedding feasts, it still offers little of guidance for those years when ecstasy will have to be translated into efficiency of family living. Therefore for the Old Testament lesson I decided (did you think the choice strange?) not upon a rhapsodic praise of love, but upon a rather prosaic description of a worthy and competent housewife.

There were problems about the choice of the New Testament lesson too. I looked at Ephesians 6, but realized immediately that you girls of twentieth century America couldn't be sold (even if I wanted to sell you) on such counsel as,

Wives, submit yourselves unto your own husbands, as unto the Lord. . . . As the church is subject unto Christ, so let the wives be to their own husbands in every thing.

Nor does Colossians 2 help very much, with its sound but limited injunction, "Husbands, love your wives, and be not bitter against them." There's no denying that St. Paul took a dim view of marriage, whether because he hadn't experienced it or because he had; and his fundamentally negative position gives us little of constructive help.

The words of our Lord himself, as reported by St. Mark, surely are more healthy and more helpful. Jesus, sharing the normal and realistic attitudes of his Jewish forebears, recognizes the existence of the two sexes as a fact in the world, and their union as the natural and proper fulfillment of their being. When he says "they twain shall be one flesh," however, he does not say that either of them becomes the other, or should become the subordinate or the slave of the other. The Christian husband will respect the integrity of his wife as a person, and the Christian wife will recognize her husband as an individual in his own right. The union is a uniting, not a suppressing; and only the free uniting of two spirits, each recognizing the individual rights of the other more than demanding his own, will make the union fruitful in a richer life for both.

Here, at once as clergyman and as sociologist, I am going to offer a few specific and practical suggestions that may trouble you now, but that I believe you'll find useful when the time comes for you to try them. One is that the right to individuality includes the right to read one's own mail, and to choose whether or not to share it. A second is that there is a sacred right to privacy of thought and feeling, into which no other person, not even husband or wife, is entitled to pry. Sharing either ideas, or letters, or emotions is real sharing only when it is done of free will; and any unilateral effort to enforce sharing will but lead to a much graver separateness of spirit.

Along with this, and in the face of a good deal of modern fondness for what is called "talking things out," I offer the proposition that disputes are not always settled most successfully by immediate discussion. Particularly at the moment when disagreement arises, we are not likely to think with clarity nor to speak with precision. An adjournment of debate now will at least permit a cooler and saner discussion later; and in my own experience I have found that often the supposed issue fades away into nothingness—and that peace has supervened without leaving any of the wounds of recrimination.

The social function of marriage is not to grant two people permission to live together, but to provide for the continuance of the human species within the guiding and protecting circle of the stable family. Because I believe the family must be stable if it is to fulfill its purpose, I can not accept the official Roman Catholic view that planning the birth of children is sinful. Both as to number and as to time of arrival in this world, the children of the future will have a better chance if they come into families that are ready and able to take care of them adequately.

But the family is incomplete without children, and the recent increase in births in families of the upper middle class is an encouraging item of statistics. Have your children as you can afford to have them, and so far as possible have them early enough so that you will be able fully to enjoy them—and they you. Bring them up in the ideals you have learned to hold dear, and by the standards you count important. Remember though, especially when the first one comes, that your husband still is in the family too; and later that the elder youngsters are going to need reassurance that they have not been superseded. Here again the Christian family will maintain its concern for every person in its membership, and never will allow any one of them to fall away into the position of an outsider.

There is so much to say that a whole series of sermons couldn't say it all. There is one last (and first) consideration that even in this brief compass may not be left out. It is that the members of a Christian marriage will be continuously and actively Christian. Nor does this mean just that they will be ethical, be good citizens, be people of good will. It means specifically that a

Christian marriage will include allegiance to the Christian Church and regular sharing in its life and work. The ideals we hold need continual stimulus; the values we profess need repeated clarifying and strengthening; the hopes we hold for ourselves and our children need a Christian community for their fulfillment.

The Church can and will give us much help that we can not do without. We who claim to be Christian owe to the cause of Christ, which is represented in the Church and carried on by it, the full loyalty of our hearts and lives. The marriage that ignores either the aid that the Church offers, or the claims that it makes, is not the marriage that will issue in spiritual creativity. Go to Church regularly. Go together. Go with your children, as soon as they are old enough. When I come to your tenth anniversary celebration, and your twentieth, you'll thank me for having given you that advice.

Reading this script over, I confess that it strikes me as being on the chilly side. It attacks romanticism, it stresses practicality, it pleads for responsibility and insists upon obligation. Yet I can't romanticize it and be honest. I can't pretend that Christian marriage operates in the rosy glow of last Saturday night's dance. I can't tell you that your delight in each other will solve all your problems. Christian marriage is an adult job, and a difficult one.

Nevertheless it is a job that can be done, and one that I pray all of you will do well. You will do it well if first you choose wisely; if then you start reverently; and if always you love unselfishly. Christian marriage "is an honourable estate, . . . and therefore is not by any to be entered into unadvisedly or lightly; but reverently, discreetly, advisedly, soberly, and in the fear of God." Those words from the marriage service say it not only for the beginning, but for all the years that are to be.

God guide your courtship. God bless your wedding. God direct your living together. God help you to bring up your children in the way that leads to fullness of life. Thus, by God's grace, your marriage will be Christian in truth.

The Lazy Liberals

28 February 1954. Psalm 139:1, 17–21, 23f.; Judges 5: 12–23; Revelation 3:14–22.

* * *

Curse ye Meroz, said the angel of the Lord, curse ye bitterly the inhabitants thereof; because they came not to the help of the Lord, to the help of the Lord against the mighty.— Judges 5:23.

I know thy works, that thou art neither cold nor hot: I would thou wert cold or hot. So then because thou art luke-warm, and neither cold nor hot, I will spue thee out of my mouth.—Revelation 3:15f.

Mr. Winthrop L. Keep has been around here a long time, and for all of that time he has been observing closely and commenting shrewdly. One morning not long ago, while he and I were stacking a load of eucalyptus logs (for which all of you who have enjoyed the fireplace at Ruddigore should thank him heartily), Mr. Keep remarked on what he felt to be the lack of energy of the more liberal Churches. "The fundamentalists," he said, "are starting new churches all over the place, while the Congregationalists and the Unitarians scarcely have made any visible progress in Oakland in the last fifty years. Why is this? And why don't you preach a sermon about it one of these days?" This then is the sermon about it: and about the larger and more general problem, which includes this specific one, of whether liberal-minded people actually are capable of real devotion and effective energy.

I have long noted that when an accusation is made against any-

one, he commonly gives not one but all of three replies. The
first is, "I didn't do it." The second is, "I did it because . . ."
The third is, "I won't do it again." That somewhat illogical pattern of response will provide a fairly satisfactory outline for our
thought this morning. The charge is that liberals are lazy. And
we shall want to ask, first, whether in fact they are lazy; then
why they are, if they are; and finally, whether they have to
be.

My first thought about Mr. Keep's immediate question, when
he put it to me that Saturday morning, was that he might be mistaken in his assumption of fact. It is true that whereas Alameda
County had only five thousand Southern Baptists fifteen years
ago, and has at least fifty thousand today, certainly more than
forty-five thousand new residents of Oakland have come to us
in those years from just the regions where the Southern Baptist
Convention has its greatest strength. The same factor of migra-
tion may be seen in the case of the even more revivalist groups,
such as the Church of God and the Pentecostal and Holiness
churches, which to a large extent reflect the normative religious
life of the less privileged strata of society in Oklahoma and
Texas; and we know that many thousands of these people came
to California in the thirties to work in the crops, and in the
forties to supply a labor force for our war industries. Thus it
might be argued that the present greater strength of fundamentalism and revivalism in this area represents not a real growth, but
merely a transfer of populations.

Furthermore, I was not sure that there was quite so great a
correlation between liberalism and laziness, locally seen, as Mr.
Keep supposed. The Unitarian Churches in Berkeley and Oakland, while not starting new units nor erecting new buildings, are
emphatically active institutions. Some Congregational and Methodist Churches in this county were liquidated during the depression; but the Congregationalists, using the designation "Community Church," have shown phenomenal growth in such new

enterprises as the Kensington Community Church at the north-
western end of the county, and the San Lorenzo Community
Church near the southeastern corner; and the Methodists have
done not at all badly with such healthy infants as their new
churches in Montclair and in Castro Valley. Similarly the
Protestant Episcopal diocese of California, which is only one of
four in this state, gave recognition to four newly established
missions at the annual diocesan convention held a month ago.

In view of the difficulty of sorting out facts and impressions,
and of the impossibility of securing precise statistics on a city or
county basis, I decided that not the local scene, but the national
one, must be examined if we were to find a sound way of measurement. Accordingly I studied the denominational reports for
the two years 1936 and 1951, the period from late depression to
postwar prosperity, and analyzed them as to relative rates of
growth in individual membership. Mr. Keep proved to be more
nearly right than I had supposed. In fact the statistics provide
overwhelming corroboration of his freehand judgment.

Roughly speaking, the more "liberal" denominations may be
identified as those affiliated with the National Council of
Churches. Of those I took eight major groups: the American
Baptists (formerly called "Northern Baptists"); the Congregational Christian Churches; the Disciples of Christ; the Lutherans,
other than the conservative Missouri Synod; the Methodist
Church; the two major Presbyterian bodies, North and South;
and the Protestant Episcopal Church. The Protestant groups outside the National Council, and in general opposed to its point
of view, are represented by the Adventist bodies, the Southern
Baptists, the Churches of God, the "Evangelistic Associations,"
the Missouri Synod Lutherans, and the Pentecostal Assemblies.
A quite different type of divergence from the National Council
pattern appears with the Unitarians and the Universalists. Finally
I recorded, for purposes of comparison, the figures for the Latter
Day Saints (that is, the Mormons) and the Roman Catholic
Church. This is what I found, for the United States as a whole:

The total population increase for the continental United States, from 1936 to 1951, had been an amazing 21 per cent. But in the same time the membership of these eighteen religious bodies had risen no less than 59 per cent. It seems that organized religion in general has been doing not badly at all.

Breaking down the total increase, however, into the four principal sectors, we learn that the increase of Unitarian and Universalist membership in the fifteen years had been 37 per cent. The Roman Catholics in the same period had gained 47 per cent. The eight National Council churches, the ones we are calling "liberal," had gone up 53 per cent. The Mormons showed a gain of 60 per cent.

Now comes a change of pace. The six Protestant groups that may be thought of as fundamentalist and revivalist reported a net increase in membership of 122 per cent. The lowest denominational gain among all the eighteen, 27 per cent, belongs to the Congregational Christian Churches; and the highest, 204 per cent, is that of the Pentecostal group. (The Southern Baptists, by the way, were not far behind that: their figure was 173 per cent.) Quite evidently Mr. Keep is right about his facts.

Nor shall I insist overmuch on some moderating factors, such as an apparent carelessness of reporting shown in the use of round numbers. It is true that figures such as 20,000, 10,000, and 50,000 don't inspire confidence in exactitude of counting; but one might discount these estimates very heavily, and still have to say that fundamentalist fervor rather than liberal tolerance seems to be making the greater headway in the religious life of America today. We liberals have been thoroughly outdone, and we may as well admit it.

What is true of these church statistics is visibly true also of our situation as a whole. Liberalism has not held its own in the contest with fanaticism, any more in the political field than in the religious. The President of the United States himself has had his hands full trying to moderate the activities of the bigots and the demagogues in his own party, and even among his own executive appointees. The idolatry of which President White spoke three weeks ago is evident throughout the country, and the melodies of moderation are almost completely unheard amid the ceaseless beating of the drums of hate.

Perhaps "lazy" is not the word; but the charge that the liberals today are not as effective as are their competitors and opponents is scarcely to be refuted by any objective evidence we can obtain within the present scene. "I didn't do it" is not an accurate reply to our question. We proceed then to the examining of "I did it because . . ." and to inquiring why things are as they are.

The basic answer is self-evident. A liberal is by definition one who thinks there may be more than one legitimate view of a given issue. He waits therefore to hear the arguments on all sides, and so he loses time. He knows that in honesty he may have to change his own mind, and so he is reluctant to bring extreme pressure to bear upon the minds of others. He is unwilling to shout down the opposition, and so he loses prestige among the multitude who hear only the loudest screaming. Neither the fundamentalist in religion nor the bitter partisan in politics is troubled by any such qualms. He is sure he is right, and so he goes straight to his business of attacking all that from his point of view is necessarily wrong.

Since you and I are liberals, we can not be like him. We would not want to be other than we are. In religion we may be ready to state our views, but we disdain any emotional orgy as a means toward getting others to share them. In politics we vote as we please, but we mount the hustings unwillingly, and we seem to weaken our case by admitting some merit in the other man's. This we regard as virtue on our part, and I believe rightly so. The other procedure we despise intellectually and detest morally, and none more heartily than does your preacher of this morning.

We ought not to be surprised, then, to find ourselves at a strategic disadvantage. The weapons on the other side include many that we could not use without surrendering our own ethical values. It follows that, at least in the short run, the unreflective in our society will be more impressed by the apparently certain than by the continually tentative. The revival meeting sweeps the adolescent of any age off his feet; and the political tirade on television, being uncomplicated by any concession to challenge or admission of doubt, gains the ready assent of those who do not think to do their thinking for themselves.

"I did it because . . ." The liberal is handicapped because he is a liberal. Recurring defeats are the price he has to pay for taking the difficult position that is his. The fundamentalist churches do gain more rapidly than the National Council ones, and the wavers of the bloody shirt often marshal more votes than do the scholars in politics. All this we should learn to expect.

It does not follow, however, that there is nothing we can do about it. The final point this morning is, "I won't do it again." Is there some way in which, without deserting our liberalism, we can serve more effectively the causes which we believe to be those of freedom, love, and truth? If I thought there were not, I not only wouldn't be preaching this sermon. If I thought there were not, there would be little point in my ever trying to preach at all.

The critical issue is that which President White expressed so clearly in his assembly speech when he returned from his Eastern trip: in his words, "that it is possible for a person to be heroic for a conditional allegiance." Too often liberalism has degenerated into indifference, and a professedly absolute loyalty to truth has become a completely befuddled and ineffective wavering among options. That whimsical but penetrating critic of our society, Lincoln Steffens, told me on his deathbed that he still wanted to write an essay on "Why Communists have to be sonsabitches." The other side of that might be a study of why ladies and gentlemen think they have to be politically, socially, and religiously null and void.

I fear most of you are too young to know the distinguished writings of archy the cockroach, mediated to an earlier generation through Don Marquis. Once archy reported a conversation with a moth, in which he had challenged the creature's evident determination to burn himself to death. The moth replied:

> it is better to be a part of beauty
> for one instant and then cease to
> exist than to exist forever
> and never be a part of beauty. . . .

Then, archy went on:

> before i could argue him
> out of his philosophy
> he went and immolated himself
> on a patent cigar lighter
> i do not agree with him
> myself i would rather have
> half the happiness and twice
> the longevity
>
> but at the same time i wish
> there was something i wanted
> as badly as he wanted to fry himself

Certainly we are not eager to fry ourselves. But is there something, is there anything, we believe in enough to gamble our whole lives on its being worth enough to live and die for? The liberal's allegiances necessarily are conditional. Can he yet be heroic for them? Surely he can; and certainly he must, if his values are at all to survive among men and women.

The first clear and essential loyalty of the liberal must be to the liberal position in its own essence. By his very insistence on hearing all sides, he is committed to seeing to it that all sides have a chance to be heard. If instead he allows his intellectual caution to sink into moral cowardice, and ceases to speak for freedom because there are those with whom freedom is unpopular, he is a traitor to his own fundamental creed.

Today the immediate crusade for the liberal is the crusade for the historic American freedoms, so badly endangered by the combination of a highly vocal minority and a fearfully unconcerned majority among our citizens. Unless we fight effectively for the maintenance of our liberties, we shall see the death of liberalism in our time; and we shall have been accessories to the murder. The true liberal can not and will not admit equal merit between liberty and tyranny, democracy and dictatorship, individual expression and enforced conformity. If for a moment we have been lazy here, we stand condemned. If for a moment we are lazy on this point from now on, we have no right to complain if our silence shall become not optional but compulsory.

Beyond the specific issue of freedom itself, the liberal faces the still more difficult responsibility, in every area, of contending for that which he knows may turn out to be wrong, but for which he must contend unremittingly as long as in his considered judgment he counts it to be right. This is the nature of true faith as distinct from unexamined dogma, alike in the field of religion and in that of politics. The possibility that we may be mistaken is always there; but it does not excuse us from the duty to do the best we know, and to do it with all our might.

As we estimate the positions of the dogmatic atheist and the excited fundamentalist, they are both in error. Since this is our position, there is no release for us from declaring our faith in God so clearly and so eagerly that others will pay attention; and there is no escape from our obligation to assert the claims of an informed and enlightened study of the documents of the Bible and the experiences of the historic Christian Church. Even while we are proclaiming our views, we shall continue for ourselves to inquire into their validity; but if they are our views, and if truly we are committed to them, we shall not deny to others the opportunity to learn of them and to come to share them. Evangelism, the preaching of the Gospel, need be no monopoly of the ignorant and the fanatic. Evangelism is the sober obligation of those who think themselves sober, and the more so because their task is the more difficult one.

In the same way the liberal will not eliminate himself from the political scene. He will speak not only for the general freedoms, but also for those specific policies and procedures which his judgment commends to him as being wise and good; and the more loudly when they are the less popular. Just because he does think those procedures wise and good, he is cowardly if he leaves them undefended, and therefore he is criminally guilty if by his silence the stupid and the evil win the victory over the public mind. Again the liberal is at a competitive disadvantage; and again this is a reason not for his doing less, but precisely one for his doing more.

What of the outcome? Let us remember that, even if we do do our best, we still may be defeated. That famous title of Dr. White's, "Education for Catastrophe," never was more applicable than it is today. If the trends we have observed this morning should continue, authentic Christianity well might be swallowed up in illiterate sentimentalism, and American freedom in a new kind of American fascism. There is so little time, and the army of the liberals always is a small one.

It need not be a discouraged army, but its soldiers must be fully realistic as they enter upon the battle. We still can lose. That we have to realize. With that we have to reckon. Can we yet keep on fighting?

We can, and we must. We can because we believe in the right as we see it, and we must because we are committed to that right with all our minds and all our hearts. Once more there is no option, unless we admit that we don't really believe and don't really care.

If that is the case with us, we live among the inhabitants of Meroz and under the everlasting curse. If that is the case, we belong to the lukewarm church of the Laodiceans, and our God will have none of us. Let us rather come to the help of the Lord against the mighty. Let us kindle anew that inward fire which first will warm our own spirits, and then will set alight the lives of those around us.

To seek, to strive, *not* to find, and not to yield. That is a truer word than Tennyson's. We may never find the Holy Grail. But we shall not shirk the quest, and we shall make no peace with the dragons that line the way. Are the liberals lazy? Not if they live the freedom which they say they love.

The Arrogant Intellectual

21 March 1954. Psalm 30:1–3, 6f., 10f.; Job 12:1–25; Romans 12:1–21.

*　　*　　*

Judge not, that ye be not judged. . . . Why beholdest thou the mote that is in thy brother's eye, but considerest not the beam that is in thine own eyes?—St. Matthew 7:1, 3.

Whosoever shall say to his brother, Raca, shall be in danger of the council: but whosoever shall say, Thou fool, shall be in danger of hell fire.—St. Matthew 5:22.

Frances Carter has supplied for us today not only the sermon topic, but also both of our texts: the former of them directly, the other by a secondary but unmistakable reference. Her postcard reads: " 'Judge not.' (those who pride themselves on being 'critical' and have no fear of calling their fellow men fools)." Since Frances is at once a Ph.D. of the University of California, a member of its staff in a highly specialized scientific department, and a regular member of the congregation of this College chapel, it is evident that she is speaking of a type of mind with which she has become familiar in academic circles. I assume I am right in having chosen "The Arrogant Intellectual" as a title to fit her subject.

Now let us face it at the outset. All of us here in this company are intellectuals in the eyes of the general public; and by much of that public we are automatically classified as intellectual snobs. As to the adjective—well, did you see today's *Tribune* announcement of this service? I quote: "Mills College Chapel, 11 A.M.

Dr. George Hedley, 'The Arrogant Intellectual.' " This morning, therefore, we are thinking first about ourselves.

Moreover, I am going to begin by offering some defense of intellectuality, and it may be in part for a kind of arrogance as well. The words that Jesus used in our texts are tricky ones, and susceptible of more than one definition. What do we mean by the verb "to judge"? What is it, exactly, to be "critical"? And what precisely is the signification of the word "fool"? We need to be sure what our terms imply, and under what conditions, before we may proceed safely to praise or to condemn.

It is clear enough that in the Sermon on the Mount Jesus was speaking often (as indeed his general habit was) in hyperbole. The paragraph which begins with "Judge not" includes also the verse about the mote and the beam; and we don't get the force of that at all until we recognize that the "beam" is no beam of light, but a roof timber: "the log," says the Revised Standard Version. Manifestly there is something extreme about the picture of a man with a log in his eye; and there can be extremes in trying to interpret the injunction, "Judge not."

To begin with, "Judge not" certainly is not to be understood as recommending that we should be neutral about moral issues. The whole drive of the gospel ethic is toward decisive judgment between right and wrong, and vigorous action not only for what is right but against all that is evil as well. The Christian is called to identify the difference without favor, and to act on that difference without fear.

Nor am I willing to concede that "Judge not" is a total rule in the field of the intellect either. In the present text of St. Matthew the passage which warns about saying "Thou fool" is followed immediately by the injunction, "Cast not your pearls before swine." Dr. J. M. P. Smith, in his classes at the University of Chicago, used to start impulsively to scribble Hebrew words on the blackboard; then stop himself, lay down the chalk, and say, "I shall not cast pearls."

Judgment is discrimination, and the honest mind must seek ever to distinguish among the very different categories of truth and probability and possibility and falsehood. The intellectual is not only entitled to demand a distinction between knowledge and ignorance, and one between sense and nonsense. He is positively required to make those distinctions for himself, and to insist on their being made by others.

"Criticism" likewise is a two-edged word. The sense in which Frances uses the adjective "critical" (rightly she puts it in quotation marks) is the popular one, connoting a wholly negative approach. Strictly speaking, however, criticism is nothing other than judgment, and so it must move through the whole field between negative and positive as the critically evaluated data may demand. The Greek of our "Judge not" text is *Me krinete*, from the verb *krino*, "I judge," which is the direct source of the Greek adjective *kritikos* and its English equivalent "critical."

Criticism as careful discrimination is integral not only to ordered thinking, but also to the maintaining of a decently civilized society. Without criticism we would have no way of distinguishing truth from lies, sense from nonsense, wisdom from folly. That means that especially in a democracy we need the critic to weigh issues, to question propaganda, to challenge prevailing prejudice. "Judge not" may not be for us a command not to know black from white.

Similarly there is much to be said for recognizing and asserting the existing foolishness of fools. There are the biologically conditioned fools to begin with, those whom we have learned to identify by the Greek-derived term "moron." (You Sopho-mores will remember the force of the *moros* half of your own class appellation.) The moron, through no fault of his own, simply doesn't have the capacity for abstract thinking. He is not to be blamed for that; but neither is he safely to be entrusted with decisions that require an independent working out of problems in logic.

There are, in addition to these aments, whose minds are lacking, those in our society who exhibit themselves as being dements, people whose minds are out of order. Their brains were good enough originally, but they have deteriorated either by shock, by strain, or by sheer disuse. I don't suppose the people whom one hears being interviewed over the radio by "sidewalk reporters" all are morons in the technical sense. But the evident unconcern of many of those people with facts, their disregard of the American tradition of fair play, their substitution of intense feeling for careful inquiry, mark them as fools in politics and as dangers to the survival of our historic freedoms. To deny their foolishness is at once to reject the evident data, and to surrender intelligence to the onslaught of the thoughtless.

Be patient, then, with the intellectual, when he seems to be arrogant. Before you condemn him wholly, ask just what he is using his intellect on, and just what he is being arrogant about. If he really is working out a judgment between right and wrong, if he is defending accuracy against error, if he is recognizing stupidity and intellectual sloppiness where they do exist, he is to be commended rather than condemned. As an intellectual I claim the right to inquire, to judge evidence and to express my judgment of it, to call folly foolish whenever I can spot its foolishness in the light of objective criticism. If this be arrogance, make the most of it.

Yet Jesus said, "Judge not," and he warned that they who called their fellows "fools" were themselves candidates for the rubbish heap of Gehenna, which was the flaming foulness of the Jerusalem city dump. The post card which started this inquiry implies the same negatives. Something seems to be wrong, after all, in judging, in being critical, in saying *"Moré!"* "You fool!" Having insisted on the importance of intelligent criticism, having demanded that folly be set apart clearly from wisdom, are we now to say that the judge and the critic are themselves at fault?

Who would venture to deny it, especially when one lives on a campus and associates daily, hourly, with high-powered intellectuals? Today's question struck a responsive chord in me as soon as I read it, for the problem has bothered me since first I met my first sixth-former when I was a lowly fag in the lower third. It bothered me so much through the years that finally I wrote a book about it, shooting particularly at those who in their intellectual arrogance thought to dismiss religion as unworthy of their notice, let alone of their respect or participation. Yes, our colleges and universities are favorite pastures of those who, in their pride, "have no fear of calling their fellow men fools."

The first point that must be made here is that the critical are required truly and accurately to criticize, and the intellectuals to use their intellects responsibly. This means, immediately, that we must recognize that in this day of intense specialization no one is qualified to be a universal doctor. I sat (and didn't you?) not only in wonderment but also decidedly in bewilderment at the assembly where Dr. Wistar told us some of the things that had happened in the world of science in the single year of 1953. I still have only the foggiest notion how nuclear fission occurs, and I simply do not understand how the fusion of hydrogen atoms can produce the violently explosive force which already our experimenters have achieved.

Because I don't know enough of the facts in these areas, I comprehend the processes scarcely at all. What my critical judgment does tell me is that this Associate Professor of Chemistry is an intelligent man, and strikingly well informed in the fields to which he has devoted his primary attention. I therefore am willing to take his word for what he tells me in the realm of his own specialties; and I shan't even ask him whether he said that the force of the hydrogen bomb equals that of twenty million tons of TNT, or twenty billion. For my purposes anything over a couple of ounces of that stuff has about the same devastating significance. Mr. Wistar has a perfect right to call me a perfect fool if I try to make any pronouncements about physical science; and I am only being scientific about myself when I readily concede him that right.

I would, however, that all of us who call ourselves scholars could develop a due humility in dealing with all the fields that are not our own. The temptation in the other direction is tremendous, and not always is it successfully resisted. Too often a physical scientist sees fit to pontificate about politics, as if his clarity about the atom gave him penetrating vision of all the ceaseless inner motion of those strange, disharmonious entities called the Republican and Democratic parties. Too often an artist thinks that his own limited and limiting financial experiences have told him all there is to know about the fluctuations of the business cycle, and so have qualified him to prescribe an economic panacea. Too often, likewise, an expert in a factual realm assumes that his categories of experiment and demonstration are enough to reveal the total and ultimate truths of the universe.

Since controlled experiment and logical demonstration can not do anything of the sort, and since these categories are the only ones this type of man recognizes as valid, he leaps to the conclusion that no ultimate truth exists beyond the reach of telescope and microscope. The error lies not in his scientific observation, which so far as it goes is accurate enough. It arises rather from his supposing that there is only this one way in which to observe; and that simply isn't so. "There are more things in heaven and earth, Horatio,/Than are dreamt of in your philosophy." And if philosophy doesn't give all the answers (and I believe the faculty of that Department will agree that it doesn't), a fortiori the necessary bounds of physical and biological science stand still further distant from the illimitable ranges of the final truth.

Perhaps there should be inserted here, at least for the record, a warning against the correlative arrogance of the unintellectual and the anti-intellectual. I think, for example, of the girl who said, after I had discussed in a lecture the evident literary dependence of the Gospels of St. Matthew and St. Luke upon that of St. Mark, "I just don't agree with you." No doubt it was her right to disagree with me and my opinions. But it is no one's right to deny manifest facts, physical or historical or literary; and when in the name of religion one attempts such a denial he is basing his religion upon a not unconscious lie.

The most notable example of this in our time is the still continuing hue and cry about evolution. In an opinion test which I have given a total of five times in the past year, twenty-three student nurses at Highland Hospital, out of a total of fifty-seven, recorded their disbelief in the evolutionary hypothesis. And before you get too horrified about the picture down at Highland, let me add that last fall eight out of thirty-nine Mills College sophomores expressed the same negative judgment. "Poor things," you say, "they don't know any better." True enough; but what they are reflecting is the arrogance of an ignorant clergy, whose members think to speak with authority of realms in which they have no right to an opinion because they have not acquainted themselves with the relevant data.

This brings us straight back to the other side. Granting that the scientist is understandably and reasonably annoyed when an ignoramus impudently sets aside two centuries of research in genetics, we still—and therefore must—deny the scientist any right to set aside, without patient and persistent individual scrutiny, four thousand years of the Hebrew-Christian tradition. Does he know, for example, that the voice of the anti-evolutionists is not the authoritative voice of the Church? If he doesn't, he is as blankly ignorant of religion as the radio revivalists are of science, and as susceptible to their propaganda as are the most unlearned of their disciples; and he ought to impose on himself a decent silence until he has made some sort of investigation. Does he know that religion has its own scholarship, exacting and objective and unceasingly self-critical? If he doesn't, he is willfully ignoring evidence which is all around him; and so he is being, in the precise meaning of the word, unscientific.

Past this, the intellectual who rejects religion, and holds it in contempt, needs to learn that there is more than one set of categories with which every man must deal. There is fact, and there is also truth. There is knowledge, and there is also faith. There is demonstration, and there are also values. They who avoid fact and knowledge and demonstration are going to do a lot of stumbling in their lives. They who avoid truth and faith and values are stumbling also, and into even deeper and much more dangerous chasms.

What matters most in human life is just that which can not be measured by mathematical method, and proved in laboratory experiments, and accepted at secondhand from an authority other than one's self. What matters most is value; and value by its nature is of the realm of faith and of active individual commitment. One can dodge these unseen entities no more than he can dodge the fact of the atom bomb. If anyone thinks to, he but sails the sea of life without a rudder and without a goal. Exactly like the ignorant denier of science, the unreflective denier of values is piling up grievous troubles for himself. To none more than to those who willfully reject the indemonstrable ultimates does the apostle give his warning, "Let him that thinketh he standeth take heed lest he fall."

There is a second kind of intellectual arrogance which Jesus condemns, and most explicitly. It is that which is turned toward persons as distinct from ideas. It is one thing to say that astrology is foolishness. It is quite another to say to the reader of astrological magazines, "You fool." It is permissible, and necessary, to discriminate critically between right and wrong. It never is in our province to hurl angry condemnation upon the wrongdoer. "Vengeance is mine: I will repay, saith the Lord." Yet the Lord himself, who knows the most about our sinfulness, is he to whom we turn for the forgiving of our sins.

What shall we do about the fool? If he is a fool in the technical sense—that is to say, a moron—we shall regret his unfortunate combination of genes, and we shall do our best to make him happy in one of those rather numerous occupations in which a limited mind is no bar to useful service and individual contentment. If he is a fool by circumstance—that is, by ignorance or by intellectual carelessness—we shall do all we can to educate him better, and when it is necessary we shall exert all our energies to outvote him. But we shall act always in sympathy rather than in anger, and in creative hope rather than in despairing contempt.

We'd better act in sympathy, for we are enough like the fool to be at one with him in many particulars. He can't extract square root? But, oh, what a fool I look to him when I try to chop down a tree! She won't miss a Liberace program on TV? Is she necessarily worse off than the hypercritical pianist who can't let herself admit that she is impressed by Rubinstein? They're suckers for the noisy demagogue? Is it just possible that some politicians have fooled some of us some of the time?

All men are not created equal; and, even more surely, not all men and women have had, or have, equal opportunity. To deny this is to equate ignorance with knowledge, and to put stupidity on a par with wisdom—and so to be ignorant and stupid on our own account. But the best mind on the Mills campus is fallible, and the most informed person in this congregation is an illiterate in every field he hasn't studied at firsthand. Remember relativity, then, and be duly humble.

In this proper humility we shall be ready at last to see the greater truth: which is that all of us are so far below the goodness and the wisdom of God that we are ultimately indistinguishable one from another. We have it in common that God made us. We have it in common that we have sinned, and come short of his glory. We have it in common, thank God, that he loves us all and calls us all to serve him.

If the intellectual lives up to his job and his opportunities, he won't have any time or energy left to expend on personal contempt. There is so much he still needs to learn in his own chosen field of inquiry. There is so much in other fields of scholarship that he would benefit by knowing, if only on the say-so of the specialists there. There is so much in the realm of values that he must explore for himself, or leave his very soul in jeopardy. If truly he sets his mind to work on the facts of life, and his heart on the values, neither mind nor heart will get around to pouring scorn on people. "Thou fool": he who says it is indeed in danger of hell fire, for he is wasting the strength he should be devoting to the quest of truth and right.

Be intellectual, I beg of you. Use your minds, inform them, stimulate them. Be critical. Distinguish sharply between sense and nonsense, and never let yourself be overborne by popular tumult. But be not arrogant, be not proud. The bell of failure tolls also for thee; and it tolls a final death knell for all whose critical faculty denies the worth of persons. There still are logs in our eyes. Our first duty is to pry them out. Then, please God, we can work rightly on the specks that seem to obscure another's vision.

Can We Go It Alone?

14 March 1954. Psalm 102:1–4, 7f., 11–13; I Kings 19: 9–18; Colossians 2:1–10.

* * *

I have trodden the winepress alone; and of the people there was none with me.—Isaiah 63:3.

He that loveth father or mother more than me is not worthy of me: and he that loveth son or daughter more than me is not worthy of me.—St. Matthew 10:37.

Those are stern texts, and it is a stern question that Lois Fink has raised for us on this Lenten Sunday morning. These are the topics as she put them on her post card:

1. How to "go it alone" and not be apart.
2. How to "go it alone" after having been together.

Neither of these is easy, but the second is the easier of the two. Let's start with that, and follow on afterward to the more difficult paradox of the former.

It is together that we begin life. There is mother first for each of us, and "ma-ma" usually is the first word in the baby's vocabulary. Then there is the immediate family circle: father, brothers, sisters, and perhaps an adoring grandmother and a fabulously entertaining uncle. The circle widens next to the block, which for small children is a social unit of major importance; and nowadays there is the nursery school, a community drawn from a wider base but brought closely together in daily association.

133

For a time, perhaps especially in the junior high-school years, the age group almost completely supersedes the family as the major focus of interest and loyalty. The necessity of belonging, the requirement of conformity to the prevailing patterns of behavior, interests, speech, and dress, dominate our life in the early teens; and any effort by parents to resist this social dictation is likely to result in grave unhappiness both for them and for a confused and divided young heart. Nowadays the adolescent pattern enforces and sharpens togetherness even more, by its demand that in order to have full status in the group one must be "going steady" with a particular one of its members.

On through senior high school and college the groupings shift more or less, but the picture is essentially the same. Clubs, cliques, fraternities and sororities, here at Mills loyalties first in the hall and then in the major department: all of these provide the in-groups without which a man is a maverick and a girl is a figure of pathos. Then comes the setting up of the new family, with all that that involves of sharing alike in effort and in delight. No one escapes the need of close human association, and happily no one is quite without some fulfilling of that need. Most people, in fact, go through life so completely involved in togetherness that going it alone is scarcely a problem for them.

What, then, makes anyone break away? Why is it that some are apart after having been thus together? One reason, and a bad one even though often it is real enough, we can note briefly and then dismiss. That is sheer selfishness. When anyone centers his attention entirely on himself within his group, his fellows grow weary very soon, and soon begin to exclude him. His pride in himself leads him then to make a virtue of necessity, and he dramatizes himself as a lonely but striking figure, standing out boldly from a blur of undistinguished and indistinguishable nonentities. Often he puts on a fairly convincing act, perhaps even persuading himself for part of the time. But he is a pathetic character in life's drama rather than an authentically tragic one, and the outcome for him is not likely to be happy.

The difference between the aloneness of the selfish and the arrogant, and that which may develop for deeper and better reasons, is a subtle one. It is difficult to define in words, and perhaps even more difficult to identify in our living. At the risk of seeming now to support some of the arrogant and the selfish in their self-deception, I think we shall have to say that aloneness may be due also to the possession of character and brains: of brains enough to see through popular stupidities, and of character enough to be forced to repudiate popular sins against God and man.

This clearly was the case with Elijah, whose solitary flight to the desert followed upon his solitary stand against Jezebel, the Syrian princess who had married the Israelite king, and who herself had become the real and tyrannical ruler of the land. "I, even I only, am left," Elijah protested; but he gave no thought to gaining a majority by surrendering his own position. And soon he was to go back and, still alone, to condemn the king whose greed transgressed the traditional property rights of the Israelite farmer Naboth.

This was the case more than two centuries later with Jeremiah, a man who was a minority of one against first his fellow priests of the little hill town of Anathoth, then the priesthood of the Jerusalem Temple, then the royal court of Judah, and finally the whole of a hysterically fear-crazed nation. I thought of using Jeremiah 15 as the first lesson for today, but decided rather to quote from it now:

Woe is me, my mother, that thou hast borne me a man of strife and a man of contention to the whole earth! . . . O Lord, thou knowest . . . know that for thy sake I have suffered rebuke. . . . I sat not in the assembly of the mockers, nor rejoiced: I sat alone because of thy hand. . . . Why is my pain perpetual, and my wound incurable, which refuseth to be healed?

Thus also might have spoken practically every one of the great prophets from Samuel to Jesus of Nazareth, from the days of King Saul to those of King Herod. The prophets were minority men because, in the face of majority unwisdom and corruption, they could be no other. We do not know just who wrote the 63rd chapter of the present book of Isaiah, nor exactly when; and it may be that the reference here was originally not to a human individual, but to the solitary grandeur and power of the Lord God himself.

Nevertheless the vivid picture it suggests is one that fits all those whose minds and hearts force them to break from the ways of the surrounding world. Treading the winepress was a social activity of major consequence and communal joy in practically all the ancient cultures. One remembers Lord Macaulay's lines in his "Horatius":

> And in the vats of Luna
> This year the must shall foam
> Round the white feet of laughing girls
> Whose sires have marched to Rome.

Here in the prophet's vision there are no laughing girls, and here there is no joy in fellowship: "I have trodden the winepress alone; and of the people there was none with me."

Jesus also spoke of such voluntary self-exclusion, and he could speak of it wittingly because he had found he had to live it. "He that loveth father or mother more than me is not worthy of me." Personal popularity is pleasant, and a public person always enjoys it and wants it. Genuine membership in a community of equals is worth still more, and every normal man or woman hungers for this. But principle may force us to surrender popularity, and an ideal firmly held may send our fellows sweeping past us unheeding if not contemptuous. The aloneness of the honest mind and the faithful conscience is not to be escaped, if dishonesty and unfaith are the prices we would have to pay for remaining together.

Yet ever we must be very sure which value is which, and whether it is the real value of fidelity or the false one of arrogance which sets us apart. I own I like cats, and that I do not share Mr. Kipling's distaste for the cat who "walks by his wild lone, waving his wild tail." But I must admit that the cat seems to be moved thus not by conscience but by self-sufficiency, and therefore that his aloneness is a denial not of an evil world but simply of a friendly community.

Cats and prophets both are solitary. We may be solitary too. If we are, we must determine whether it is really because we are prophets, or whether it is just because we are cats.

We may be alone after having been together. We may have to be, for the sake of God and truth and justice. And if we have to be we can be, so long as justice and truth and God come first among our values. This is why Jesus was alone in Gethsemane, and on the cross. This is why he knew, and told his followers, that the sword of conscience might on occasion have to sever the idle peace of ordinary human comradeship.

Lois rightly does not leave the problem there. Her first subject, and her critically important one, is "How to 'go it alone' and not be apart." An adequate solution of this issue will resolve also the distinction between the cat's aloneness and the prophet's, between the solitary who is alone because he worships himself and the one who is alone because he is willing to surrender himself to the higher good. The next lines after our text in St. Matthew are these:

He that taketh not his cross, and followeth after me, is not worthy of me. He that findeth his life shall lose it: and he that loseth his life for my sake shall find it.

It is integral to the view of Jesus, and to the Christian judgment throughout the centuries, that the kind of aloneness which alone is justified, and which is morally inevitable, comes not from self-confident contempt of humanity, but from the expression of the love of God in one's own loving devotion to the well-being of every man and woman. We seek to shun stupidity, but we may not hold the stupid in despite. We must hate evil, and we shall make no peace with oppression; yet the Christian will continue to love the evildoer, and to care desperately for the saving of the very oppressor as well as of those who are oppressed.

Togetherness for the Christian therefore is much more than a matter of the family bond and of close personal acquaintance. It is a question of his attitude to all the world of humankind. The first time I was in New York City, as a very young graduate student, I was more alone than ever I had been before in my life. I was dazed by the rushing traffic; I was harassed by the ceaseless noise; I was resentful of the standard New York pattern of brusque discourtesy. I had a whole week end open in which to see the big town; but after a day and an evening of unhappy wandering, a solitary Ishmael in the desert waste of Broadway and Forty-second Street, I fled by the New Haven back to the quiet open spaces of the Boston Public Garden.

Since then I've learned a few things, and among them that there is a difference between being alone and being lonely: or, in Lois's terms, that one can be alone without being apart. Aloneness is a matter of fact and circumstance. Loneliness is an individual, emotional, and essentially selfish reaction to that fact.

The day before I wrote this sermon was one on which I treated myself to half a day off. I was alone in San Francisco among something like a million people, and until a favorite head waiter greeted me at dinnertime I saw no one whom I identified as ever having seen before. But I found profound content in being one of the sidewalk throng on Market Street; I happily violated good social welfare usage by giving quarters to a couple of old cadgers within half a block of the Palace Hotel; and I joined delightedly in the giggles over the new scramble-amble crossings in the financial district. Alone I was, and wholly unimportant; but not apart, for I knew my full and active membership in the whole mass of unimportant but united men and women.

"The crowd is the spectacle," says Robert Bridges of an English football game;

> its wrestle and agony
> is more than the actors, and its contagion so thick
> and irresistible that ere (one) feel surprise
> he too may find himself, yea philosophy and all,
> carried away . . . he will feel his spirit
> drawn into kinship and their exaltation his own;
> the more that he himself can be no part thereof,
> incomprehensible because comprehending.

It may be that the more we understand people and their motivations, the less most of them will understand us. The thoughtful inquirer is incomprehensible to those who never ask questions, and the eager seeker for new good is a pain in the neck to those who unreflectively accept the *status quo*. Yet this situation permits us neither to yield to all the standards and shibboleths of the mass, nor to repudiate the mass as beneath us and unworthy of our respect. The task ever is to be alone when we must be for conscience' sake, but to have such a conscience that we never shall betake ourselves apart from our human world.

Alone without being apart? There is yet one answer that includes them all. It is that one man and God constitute a majority: or one woman and God, no less. "Be strong and of a good courage," says the Lord to the young General Joshua, who has been assigned to an invasion command for which he feels himself inadequate. "Be strong and of a good courage, for I the Lord thy God am with thee withersoever thou goest."

When we find ourselves alone among mankind, the one question we must answer honestly and accurately is whether we are thus alone because we have chosen to be with God. If rightly we can answer "Yes," then we have substituted a greater togetherness for a smaller one. This is the togetherness that made Joshua a victor, and Jeremiah a hero, and Jesus of Nazareth the Saviour of the world.

This is a togetherness that will not take us apart from men, however much we may differ from the human majority. The God who calls us to distinguish ourselves from the mass calls us also to join the mass and to serve it. For his sake we may have to tread the winepress alone, and to know that of the people there are none with us. For his sake we may find ourselves at variance even with those of our own households. And so we shall be alone; but we shall not be apart.

We shall be alone, but we shall not be lonely. We shall not be lonely because still our hearts are bound in love to all God's children. We shall not be lonely because ever our hearts are sustained by the love of God himself. Can we go it alone? Sometimes we must, in this human world. But we shall not be lonely; for God is with us whenever we are brave enough to be with God.

SOME QUESTIONS OF THEOLOGY

Arguing with Atheists

Who or What Is the Devil?

What Does the Death of Jesus Mean?

Did Jesus Go to Hell?

Is There Health in Us?

Arguing with Atheists

28 November 1954. Psalm 16; Isaiah 45: 1–13; I St. Peter
3:8–17.

*   *   *

The fool hath said in his heart, There is no God.—Psalm
14:1=Psalm 53:1.

*Be ready always to give an answer to every man that asketh
you a reason of the hope that is in you, with meekness
and fear.*—I St. Peter 3:15.

*Without faith it is impossible to please him: for he that
cometh to God must believe that he is, and that he is a
rewarder of them that diligently seek him.*—Hebrews 11:6.

Lilabeth Galbraith couldn't wait to mail her sermon-subject
post card to me. On that morning in October when the cards
first were distributed with the leaflets, she tackled me on the
way up to Ruddigore. During the summer, she said, she had had
a number of discussions with people who didn't believe in God;
and I gather that she was not wholly satisfied with the way they
had come out. "What does one say in that sort of situation?" she
asked. I promised her that I'd try to think of something to say,
and that I'd say it as soon as I could. Here we are, then, with
Lilabeth's question: "How should one argue with an atheist?"

There is a prior question, however; and that is whether it is
profitable to argue with an atheist at all. This really depends not
so much upon the nature of atheism as it does upon the nature

of the individual who claims to be an atheist. Our tradition is
full of folk sayings that warn against wasting much breath on
some people: "There's none so blind as he that won't see";
"Convince a man against his will, he's of the same opinion still";
and "I'm willing to be convinced, but I'd like to see the man
that can convince me."

There can be a kind of devotion to atheism that is just as
emotional, just as irrational, just as adamant, as ever was the
religious fanaticism of the most naive of frontier sectarians. All
of us have met people whose atheism is like this; and in time we
have learned that, while debating with them is likely to generate
a lot of heat, it seldom produces much light either for them or
for ourselves. This sort of intense and wholly subjective atheism
seems often to be the product of some unhappy experience in
childhood or youth. Sometimes it is a reaction against some
relative or acquaintance who was personally religious, but who
also was personally hated; and the hatred easily was carried over
from the individual to that individual's faith. Another cause may
be an intense personal tragedy, out of which the sufferer has
come convinced that there is no justice in the universe, and that
therefore there can be no power of intelligence and good will
at its center: that is to say, that there can be no God.

Probably it would take a psychiatrist to identify the real
causation in cases such as these; and even if he did bring the
cause to the level of the patient's consciousness he would not
necessarily destroy thereby the structure of rationalizations and
clichés that during the years have been built up around it. Certainly mere disputation will get nowhere in disposing of attitudes that have been created in the realm of the unconscious.
Usually it doesn't take long, and it doesn't take a lot of psychological training, to identify the kind of atheism which, not
being based on reason, can not be overthrown by reason. When
we do identify it, we may as well decide not to argue in words,
to no profit. What's left for us here is simply to demonstrate in
our lives, and to pray that the atheist's life may be turned into

happier channels than those which have brought him to where
he is today.

My own guess would be that the type of atheist I have been
describing, and with whom I think it's almost totally useless to
argue, represents a majority of those who are at all aggressive
and emphatic in saying they don't believe in God. But there are
others, whose way of thinking is less conditioned by emotional
experiences, who are quite positive about being negative in this
realm. I think they are not hopeless cases, by any means; and
for our contacts with them Lilabeth asks a question which is
fully pertinent. What has the believer in God to say, legitimately and rationally, to the man who holds such belief to be
irrational and therefore illegitimate?

The first reply ought to be a question. We need to learn from
our atheist friend just how he defines this God whose existence
he denies. Very often it turns out that he doesn't believe in a
long-bearded gentleman sitting on a throne in a physical heaven,
reaching his hand down now and then to interfere with and
upset the lives of men and women. And usually this man is quite
surprised to discover that no competent theologian believes such
nonsense either. If you ask people of this sort whether they
think there is order and purpose in the universe, they not infre-
quently will say, "Why, yes, of course." If you go on then to
ask whether that order and purpose spring from a conscious,
intelligent being, again you're likely to get an affirmative response.

When this is the trend of the conversation, you are entitled
at once to point out that your worthy opponent is not an
atheist at all, but merely an ignoramus. It isn't God he is denying, but simply an infantile concept of God that any sensible
person should have discarded about the time he changed from
three wheels to two. Anyone who identifies faith in God with a
kindergarten grasp of the problem is simply announcing that he
never should have been promoted to the first grade. It might be
putting it a bit extremely to say that no one has a right to call

himself an atheist unless and until he has taken a full three-year course in a graduate school of theology, so that he may have some notion what sort of God this is whose existence he presumes to deny. But it certainly is not extreme to insist that the professed atheist shall define his terms precisely, and that he shall discuss the issue not on a preschool but on an adult level.

We who do believe need a special caution here. If we hold that the atheist ought to know just what he's talking about when he rejects God as a possibility, then even more do we need to know what we're talking about when we affirm God as a reality. If our own ideas of God are juvenile, they will prove to be indefensible in grown-up conversation; and the beating we'll take will be one that we shall thoroughly deserve. Manifestly not many of you are going to go through a full theological seminary course. But if you count yourselves to be believers, you are obligated not only to think through the meaning of your belief, but to think it through with the aid of the great thinkers of our tradition from the time of—well, say Isaiah in the seventh century B.C.—on to Karl Barth and Reinhold Niebuhr in our own day. Unless we do this, we are just as incompetent to discuss the matter as is the least informed of our professedly atheist friends.

Let us assume, then, that we have surmounted this first obstacle of definition. Let's say that you and your antagonist have agreed that God doesn't have a beard, doesn't live in a golden palace somewhere in the sky, doesn't operate by incalculable whimsy; but that you disagree, clearly and frankly, on whether there is either a conscious planner of the universe, or a conscious power within it: a power, not our own, that makes for righteousness. As I recall our conversation on the geranium path, Lilabeth said she had been talking with young scientists who maintained that they couldn't believe in God because they could explain everything in terms of natural process.

This is another area in which the religious person, unless he is very careful about his own thinking, is likely to be betrayed into a position he can't maintain against an able debater. To say that the beauty of the sunset proves the existence of God may be poetry, but it certainly isn't serious argument; and we can't blame the spokesman for the negative if he sees it as romantic balderdash. To say that God's intelligence is proved by the scheme of natural law isn't good argument either. Natural law is itself an inference from observation; and whatever may have caused it is not to be observed by either a telescope or a microscope.

The so-called "proofs of God" that were generally accepted in the Middle Ages were demolished almost two hundred years ago by Immanuel Kant, and they can not be regarded as intellectually convincing by anyone who knows Kant's thinking even at secondhand. The whole issue here turns on the nature of proof. What we have to realize first for ourselves, and then to get over to the doubters, is that God is not susceptible of laboratory experiment or astronomical observation. Both the nucleus of a cell and the more distant stars are invisible to the naked eye; but both of these are material objects, and both are seen by the aid of other material objects called lenses. God is not a material object, and no lens in the Life Science Building or on Mount Palomar is going to disclose him to us.

Once we admit frankly that we can't prove the existence of God in any such terms, then we are free at once to point out that the scientist can't disprove that existence either. Strictly speaking, atheism is rationally impossible because it is always irrationally dogmatic. The more honest of those who call themselves atheists will concede, when the point is forced upon them, that they are not really atheists at all but just agnostics: that is, that they simply don't know.

Hooray, then! Now we're getting together. For every honest Christian is, so far as pure intellect is concerned, a thoroughgoing agnostic too. It is well for us to reserve the terms "knowing" and "knowledge" to the zone of the physically objective and measurable, and not to confuse things by declaring that we "know" God. We do not know God in any such way as we know the greenness of chlorophyll or the wetness of water or the hardness of granite.

The word that is applicable to God, and to every concept that is not merely physical and external, is not "knowledge" but "faith." Every attitude that man can hold in the realm of the non-material and the unmeasurable is an attitude of faith. It is by faith indeed that we come to God, believing that he is; but it is just as much by faith, it is just as much without the possibility of demonstration, that others flee from God, believing that he is not. "You must wager," wrote the French scientist and mystic Blaise Pascal in the middle of the seventeenth century. "It is not optional. You are embarked. Which will you choose then?"

The word "irrational" has come commonly to mean "antirational." That last no reasonable human being has any right to be. But the reasonable man or woman will recognize that there is much in life—and all in life that matters most—that is nonrational. To quote Pascal again, "The heart has reasons of which the reason can know nothing." Love is not the creature of cold reason. Neither is good will nor honesty nor courage of heart. We can't prove the objective validity of any of these; but nevertheless we can make them the rules and the rulers of all our living.

The reason which St. Peter adjured his readers to be ready to give was a reason of the hope that was in them. The things that are seen are temporal, temporary. Only the unseen things, the things that never can be seen by the physical eye and that certainly can't be measured by calipers, are eternal in their living power. These we can choose to accept by faith, or to reject by faith; but inevitably it's faith, either way.

That brings us to the final challenge and to our ultimate answer. You and I have chosen to believe in God. We are under a solemn obligation, first, to understand just what we mean by that. We are required then to distinguish carefully between our faith in God and our knowledge of the physical world. We are entitled to insist that those who would differ from us shall define with equal care and discriminate with equal precision. But we shall not make our faith effective, nor our argument impressive, save as our faith in eternal value becomes evident in our earthly living.

Far off in the interior of China, in a village beside the Grand Canal, my father was showing slides from a stereopticon; as we called it then, a "magic lantern." Even as a small boy I knew that the pictures were pretty crude in outline and in color. But that night the people sat spellbound in the dust as on the screen there was unfolded the story of one who loved his friends so much that he gave his life for them. Three crosses flashed before us, and three men crucified: two thieves, and between them the Lord of love. All at once an old woman got up and stumbled forward on her bound feet, crying, "I always knew there must be a God like that."

Is there a God? Men and women have believed there is, because they have known no other way to account for absolute devotion to beauty, truth, and goodness, whatever may be the cost; and this is what the Christian means when he speaks of the supreme revelation of God in our Lord Jesus Christ. Is there a God? The world will believe there is, when it finds God living in those who have given themselves wholly to the doing of his will. Is there a God? Even the atheist will say, "Yes, there must be," when God really gets a chance to show himself in those who claim to be his people.

We need not discount the value of discussion where discussion is relevant. A certain amount of clear thinking, a positive demand that the issues shall be accurately defined and rightly understood, will do much to clear away old confusions and so to open the way to new realizations. But the words of argument are feeble indeed when compared with the argument of life.

You and I are of those who have chosen to believe. We are

ready to give a reason of the faith that is in us: to provide not indeed a rational proof of our conclusion, but a fully rational account of our position. Not in contempt, but in deep sorrow, we hold that he who says there is no God is a self-deluding fool. But we shall not win the doubter to our side by words alone. If truly we believe, we shall live. If genuinely we have faith, we shall not fail in action. If God is real for us, God will be real in us.

Our God is light. Then we shall spread light in the dark places. Our God is truth. Then we shall be wholly honest in ourselves. Our God is love. Then we shall give ourselves in love for all of God's children. When we do, by God's grace, it may be that American sophisticates as well as Chinese peasants will cry, "I always knew there must be a God like that."

Who or What Is the Devil?

31 January 1954. Psalm 16:1-12; Zechariah 3; St. Luke 11:14-26.

*　　*　　*

Your adversary the devil, as a roaring lion, walketh about, seeking whom he may devour.—I St. Peter 5:8.

This sermon is going to have what amounts to a triple introduction. The third part will be the identifying of the day's questioner. To that will be prefixed a story. But that story, which is a general one, must itself be introduced by some words of specific reminiscence.

Among my long, unhappy, far-off days, and battles long ago, I have to record the teaching of a single course no less than seven times within three college years and one summer session. It was a course in the life of Jesus, and the textbook was the Burton and Goodspeed *Harmony of the Synoptic Gospels*. In accordance with standard academic procedure, students commonly signalized the end of the course by selling their books; and some of those *Harmonies* passed through a number of successive hands before finally they disintegrated.

One day, during perhaps my fifth or sixth journeying through the material, I found in the classroom a copy of the book which some student had left behind. When I picked it up, it fell open at that passage in St. Luke which was today's second lesson, the parable of the evil spirit and the empty house. And in the margin I saw the penciled notation, "Here is where Hedley tells his devil story."

Really, I've told it very few times in the years that have followed, and I think never again in a "Life of Jesus" class. But it does belong at the outset of this sermon, and I'm going to tell it now. One more preface, however; namely, that I got it first from a Southern Baptist minister. That, I am sure, guarantees its orthodoxy.

The tale is that of a rural preacher who was very eloquent, but who was addicted to that locution which uses both a noun and a pronoun as the subject of a sentence: "Bill he went to town," "Mary she cooked the dinner," and so on. This preacher, according to my informant, once began a sermon thus:

"My brothers an' sisters, my tex' this mawnin is, 'The devil he goeth about as a roarin' lion, seekin' whom he may devour.' An' ah proposes to discuss this tex' under three heads; which is, fust, who the devil he was; second, where the devil he was goin'; an', third, what the devil he was roarin' about."

That, ladies and gentlemen, defines almost exactly the subject of our inquiry this morning. Our questioner is the eminent historian and philosopher of religion, my friend and colleague Elliot Diller. Onto a single post card he managed to crowd the following:

1. Is the Devil as real as God? or
2. Does evil negate divine omnipotence? or
3. Does the Devil belong in Christian theology?

And then, without a number, "Is Good absolute, and evil relative?" Lest I should be misunderstood, I shall not say that Dr. Diller knows at least as much about the Devil as I do. But I do suspect he was less in quest of information for himself than he was trying to needle me into tackling yet another difficult question. I am tackling it; but with the proviso that if my replies don't satisfy you, you go and inquire directly of the higher authority from whom the question came.

Is the Devil real? Does he belong in Christian theology? Or, in the phrasing of our announced title, "Who or what is the Devil?" What has theology to say on this? And what our own experience?

In the Bible and in later Christian literature we meet the Devil under a number of aliases, some of which we shall need to examine now. Let me point out first, however, that the snake in the Garden of Eden is not a case in point. This is not an alias, but historically a matter of mistaken identity. What the original story of Eve and the serpent tries to tell us is why people dislike snakes. All the well known theological implications rightly or wrongly were read into the tale long afterward.

There is no Hebrew word that means "Devil" in anything like our familiar sense. "Devils" appear only four times in the King James version of the Old Testament, and then always in the plural. Twice they are "goats" or "hairy ones" (*sairim*), and twice "spoilers" or "destroyers" (*shedim*). The Revised Standard Version renders the one word as "satyrs," the other as "demons." In each of the four cases the reference is to pagan sacrifices made to these beings; and in each case the Hebrew writer denies their existence implicitly or explicitly:

> They sacrificed to demons which were no gods . . .
> To new gods that had come in of late,
> Whom your fathers never had dreaded.

The better known "Satan" also is in the Hebrew writings; but he too is a late arrival, and he is far from being a major character. "Satan" really is not a proper name, but a common noun meaning "adversary." In the Hebrew it is used always with the definite article, *ha-satan*, "the adversary." This Satan is mentioned in the whole Old Testament only sixteen times, and twelve of those are in the one story which occupies the first two chapters of the book of Job.

What probably is the Satan's earliest appearance is also his most revealing one. In II Samuel 24:1, a very early account of the Israelite kingdom, we read that "The anger of the Lord was kindled against Israel, and he moved David against them to say, Go, number Israel and Judah." This taking of a census was regarded as wrongful, perhaps because it indicated trust in human numbers rather than in divine help. Anyway, it issued in heavy punishment, the death of 70,000 people from a sudden plague. And the important thing to notice is that, in this account in the book of Samuel, the Lord himself is the tempter to evil—and a highly unprincipled one, for he tempts the king just in order to have an excuse to punish the nation.

By the time the priestly authors of the books of Chronicles came along and rewrote the ancient legends, perhaps five hundred years later, their developed moral sense could not accept such unethical behavior on the part of their God. Listen now to their slight but crucial revision of the same verse, as we find it in I Chronicles 21:1: "And Satan stood up against Israel, and provoked David to number Israel." David yields, as in the earlier version, takes the census, and the seventy thousand die. Whether the Satan is either necessary or adequate as an explanation of evil we shall have to consider in a few minutes. At least we shall recognize that he is a decided improvement on a God who is himself a malicious Satan.

In the relatively late folk tale which opens the book of Job, the Satan clearly is a member of the heavenly court, and when the episode begins he is reporting back there after making a world tour. He seems to be a sort of celestial prosecuting attorney whose job is to identify and demonstrate the evil in mankind. He is anti-Job, as he is against all men. But he is definitely subordinate to God, and brings suffering upon the patient hero only with God's permission, and only for a limited time.

The remaining Old Testament references to the Satan are a single line in Psalm 109, a hymn of hate which includes, "Let Satan [or, the adversary] stand at his right hand," and the two verses in the third chapter of the book of Zechariah which you heard in this morning's first lesson. In this latter case the Satan and the angel of the Lord are contending for dominance over the high priest Joshua: and so again this is not a case of a Devil being matched against God, but of two minor functionaries who take opposite points of view.

"Lucifer" does appear once in the 1611 Old Testament, but not as the character we know so well from *Paradise Lost*. The passage is Isaiah 14:12:

How art thou fallen from heaven, O Lucifer, son of the morning! how art thou cut down to the ground, which didst weaken the nations!

But in the Hebrew the word is *helel*, "shining one," and the context shows that the reference is to the political downfall of the tyrannical and hated king of Babylon.

The first answer, then, to Mr. Diller's questioning is that Hebrew thought in the Old Testament did not suppose the Devil to be "as real as God." It didn't really give the Devil any place at all; and it is only a late Christian reading back into the texts that has seen a Devil in Lucifer, or in the Satan, or in the serpent of Eden. What then about the Christian tradition itself?

By the time Christianity was beginning to take form, popular Jewish thinking had been greatly influenced from the direction of Persia. The very essence of the Persian theology, attributed to the legendary prophet Zoroaster, was a basic dualism of good and evil. In the Zoroastrian creation story the god of light, Ahura Mazda, creates all things good and beautiful; and to balance each of these the dark and evil being Ahriman, or Angra Mainyu, promptly counter-creates a corresponding evil. Thus in the *Vendidad* Ahura Mazda tells the inquiring prophet:

The first of the good lands and countries which I created was the Aryana Vaego, by the good river Daitya. Thereupon came Angra Mainyu, who is all death, and he counter-created the serpent in the river, and winter.

The second of the good lands and countries which I created was the plains in Sughdha. Thereupon came Angra Mainyu, who is all death, and he counter-created by his witchcraft the fly which brings death to the cattle.

Thus, one by one, Ahura Mazda creates in all sixteen good lands and countries; and for each of these Angra Mainyu counter-creates an evil: the sin of unbelief, the mosquito, the sin of pride, witchcraft, oppression by foreign rulers, and last of all winter again.

Christianity never has assigned any such creative power to a Devil, and so it never has given to him anything like a position of equality with God. The New Testament writings reflect rather a combination of the Hebrew idea of the Satan, the adversary or tempter, with the generally prevailing belief in numerous supernatural evil beings who are best described as "demons." These demons seem most commonly to be the ancient gods of paganism, by late Jewish and early Christian thought degraded to lower levels of power and regarded as being wholly evil in their character. "Beelzebub," for example, whom we met in our second lesson of this morning, is simply *Baal-zebul*, "the lord of filth," or idolatry; and St. Jerome is responsible for the transcription "Beelzebub," "the lord of flies," who was the god of the ancient Philistine city of Ekron.

The word "Devil" itself comes from the Greek *diabolos*, which, like the Hebrew "Satan," means primarily "accuser," or "slanderer." Both terms are used to describe the tempter of Jesus in the wilderness, and both are employed in the same way by St. Paul. The nearest New Testament approach to the Persian view is in the book of Revelation, where the Devil is called "that old serpent," and where he is twice honored in the King James version by being spelled with a capital letter. But even here he is chiefly a tempter rather than a creator; and the last we hear of him is that "the Devil that deceived them was cast into the lake of fire and brimstone."

Really, we've made no progress at all. There is scarcely any more Devil in the New Testament than in the Old, in authentic Christian teaching than in Jewish. Certainly a Devil who is cast into the lake of fire is not at all the ruler of all Hell whom we know in late Christian mythology and in the *Inferno* of Dante Alighieri. The Scriptures, in short, do not teach that the Devil is as real as God. In this sense, then, the Devil does not belong in Christian theology.

Then (to paraphrase our opening story) what the devil is all the roaring about? Is the Devil real? Ah, yes, he is: and we meet him all too often, live with him far too much.

In a book which I had when I was about eight years old, the Devil had yet another name than Satan or Lucifer or Beelzebub. His name here was a Latin one. It was *Ipse*, and *ipse* means "self." Long years afterward I heard a gentleman ask the great preacher Dr. Charles E. Jefferson, "Sir, do you believe in the existence of a personal Devil?" Dr. Jefferson replied, "From long experience and observation, I have concluded that the Devil is distinctly personal."

The Devil is personal indeed. He is precisely *ipse*, self. Eve blamed it all on the serpent; but it was her own curiosity and her own greed that led her to eat the forbidden fruit. Immediately afterward Adam blamed it on Eve: "The woman tempted me, and I did eat." Men and women have been blaming each other ever since, and blaming the Devil too. It is time we learned to put the blame where it belongs: on *nos ipsos*, on ourselves.

What is the Devil? It is national arrogance and social snobbery. It is public corruption and private chiseling. It is treason to one's country and it is disregard of human need. It is cruelty and cowardice, perjury and pettiness, stupid reaction and selfish rebellion. Who is the Devil? He is George Hedley, and he is each one of you, whenever and inasmuch as we yield control of ourselves to any one of the forces of wrong.

But isn't God somehow to blame for allowing such evils to be in the world, and in us? He is, if blame attaches to his gift of human free will. Earlier this year I tried to point out that only the possibility of failure gives any meaning to success, that only the chance to do wrong provides any merit in the doing of right. We might have been perfect beings from the start. And if so, we would have been automata, robots, zombies. God wanted us rather to be achieving, growing, free personalities. He could effect this only by allowing us the opportunity to achieve nothing, to grow not at all, to sacrifice our freedom to the bonds of fear and laziness and self-indulgence.

God is no more our tempter than an external Devil is. The writer of the epistle of St. James, ignoring the Satan altogether, makes the charge against us directly and inescapably:

Let no man say when he is tempted, I am tempted of God: for God cannot be tempted with evil, neither tempteth he any man: but every man is tempted, when he is drawn away of his own lust, and enticed.

Our own lust, our own desires, our own self-seeking: these are the personal Devils that tempt us to evil. They are not as real as God, for we can conquer them, and so destroy them, if we but will commit ourselves to God's will and his grace. Thus evil is relative, whereas good is absolute. It is to our freedom of choosing that evil is related, and the evil in us is just as real as we choose to let it be.

That evil existing in us does not in any way deny God's power. It reflects rather God's deliberate surrender to us of the power to attain the good in our own right, and so to be persons rather than machines. God's power always is for good, including the good of our own self-direction. God's power is available also to aid us toward our achieving of the good. The necessary combination still is that of the grace of God with the self-discipline of our human spirits. Only they who make void the grace of God allow the Devil to possess their hearts.

Lucifer has reigned in us too long. Let us cast him now from his throne. Beelzebub too long has covered us with filth. Let us repudiate him, and clean up our lives. The Satan too long has deceived us by his insidious flatterings. Let us no longer heed him who is a liar and the father of lies. *Ipse*, self, has held much too much of our attention. It is time to look outside ourselves, to our fellows and to our God.

Who or what is the Devil? He, it, is the evil we have allowed to control us. He, it, will cease to be when by the grace of God we commit ourselves wholly to the good. The Devil yet walks about as a roaring lion. So long as mankind endures, our adversary will be seeking whom he may devour. It is for us to determine that he shall not devour us.

What Does the Death of Jesus Mean?

Septuagesima Sunday, 14 February 1954. Psalm 69:1–6, 17f.; Wisdom of Solomon 2:1, 12–24; I St. Peter 2:19–25.

* * *

We preach Christ crucified, unto the Jews a stumblingblock, and unto the Greeks foolishness; but unto them which are called, both Jews and Greeks, Christ the power of God, and the wisdom of God.—I Corinthians 1:23f.

God was in Christ, reconciling the world unto himself, not imputing their trespasses unto them; and hath committed unto us the word of reconciliation.—II Corinthians 5:19.

It became him, for whom are all things, and by whom are all things, in bringing many sons unto glory, to make the captain of their salvation perfect through sufferings.—Hebrews 2:10.

It is fitting that the most serious and most difficult sermon question of the year should have been raised by the chairman of the student Chapel Committee. "Just what does it mean," asked Leslie Baun one Sunday last fall, "when we say that Christ died to save us?" I promised then that I would attempt a reply when the Christmas festival was past; and on this first Sunday of the pre-Lenten season, when the altar again is decked in the purple of penitence and suffering, it is well that we should face a question which goes to the very heart of the Christian gospel.

Leslie's question is one that, within our American Christian pattern, seems to be discussed either too much or not nearly enough. With the "too much" side few of you here this morning have any personal acquaintance. It belongs to the fundamentalist, revivalist groups, in which salvation "by the blood of the Lamb" is the standard, and in some cases, the only theme of the preaching. You may possibly have met it in the form of tracts handed out on street corners or left on bus seats, typically with such headings as "Without the shedding of blood there is no remission of sin."

The frontier revivalist approach is naïve, historically uninformed, and theologically inaccurate; and it may be also psychologically and morally dangerous, if and when it exalts intense emotionalism at the cost of stability and self-control. Nevertheless it is truer to the basic Christian faith, and also to the realities of human life, than is the polite ignoring of Jesus' death which marks so many of our "good" churches in upper-middle-class neighborhoods. There is suffering in life, and there is death at life's end. Too often in our comfort we try to ignore those plain facts; and so we avoid the embarrassment, what seems to us the crudity, of centering our thought upon the suffering and death of our Lord himself.

Several years ago I found out that while the girls in the College Chorus could sing the Christmas carols and hymns readily, and in most cases from memory, scarcely any of them even remembered having heard such classics of the Christian tragedy as "In the Cross of Christ I Glory" and "When I Survey the Wondrous Cross." The same psychology of keeping on the sunny side (which really is just keeping on the sentimental side) is reflected in the standard Protestant treatment of Holy Week. We are accustomed to pass straight from Palm Sunday to Easter Day, and so from the triumphal entry of Jesus into Jersalem immediately to the triumph of the Resurrection; and still only a minority of American Protestants pause in between to recognize Good Friday, the day without which the triumph would be empty and the Resurrection impossible.

We have a service here in the Chapel each Good Friday, but

most of you are elsewhere during that spring vacation week. I urge you now to go to Church somewhere this next Good Friday, and as much as you can during the rest of Holy Week too. You need to do this, if your Christian faith is to be kept in balance and to maintain its depth; for joy without pain is fraudulent, and Christianity without the cross of Christ is meaningless. Pending the coming of that climactic week and our dispersal then, I seize this chance Leslie has afforded us, on the morning when the Church year sets our feet upon the way of the cross, to ask you to think now of what the death of Jesus means: of what it has meant in Christian history, of what it can mean and ought to mean to you and me.

What does the death of Jesus mean? Three subtopics will help us to organize our reply. What does the death of Jesus mean historically? What does it mean theologically? What does it mean personally, to us who count ourselves Christian?

The history belongs to a springtime in Palestine a little over nineteen hundred years ago. A young Jewish layman, who had become a rabbi *de facto* because he had things to say to his people, had spent something over two years as a wandering teacher. Round him there had gathered a little band of men and women, drawn first by curiosity, then held at his side by the enthralling power of an incisive mind and a direct and absolutely simple spirit. Jesus of Nazareth was a prophet in the authentic line of Nathan and Elijah, Amos and Micah, Isaiah and Jeremiah: speaking because he could not keep silent, fearless because he was assured that his message was the veritable message of the most high God.

Incisiveness, directness, simplicity: these are not often popular virtues. We don't like to have our shams pierced through, our curtains of self-deceiving torn aside. We prefer our devious rationalizings to any straightforward assertion of the truth. We cover up our problems in complexity, lest a simple approach should bring us to solutions that we might find uncomfortable and inconvenient. The true prophet therefore is usually a lonely man, and as he becomes at all widely known he is likely to be increasingly persecuted.

Thus it was with the young prophet of Galilee. He was too honest, and his message was too driving, for him or it to fit into any of the prevailing party systems of the first century. He was a Pharisee, but he had scant patience with the false Pharisaism that used the technical Law to make void the moral demands of the Almighty. He was a Jew, but he lacked the political subtlety that had made the Jerusalem priesthood compromise with Greco-Roman culture. He was a subject of Rome, but he could not render to Caesar any of the things that belonged to God.

As a conforming member of any one of these contemporary systems, Jesus would have had a ready-made group of friends and defenders. As a solitary critic of the wrong in all of them, as a single-minded spokesman for the right in each, he succeeded in confusing and therefore in antagonizing everyone who had an institutional value at stake. Society ever has demanded that its members be hundred percenters; but it never has been happy about those whose hundred per cent loyalty is to their own individual vision of the truth. Jesus was, in short, subversive; and he had to be got rid of.

That might have been achieved in several ways. He might have been intimidated into silence, but he would not hold his peace. He might have gone into exile; but on the night of his arrest he chose not to take the easy way from Gethsemane up the Mount of Olives, and over the crest into the impenetrable maze of gullies that led to the Jordan and the desert. No, he scarcely could have been imprisoned; for that would have provided that most dangerous of all threats to the *status quo*, a living martyr. What did happen was that he was killed, and that he chose to be. What does this mean, in terms of the events as they are recorded?

Once a theological student said to me, "It wouldn't make any difference if Jesus had died of a bad cold." Ah, but it would. The mind of Jesus was brilliant; the spirit of Jesus was compelling;

the love of Jesus was a joy to all who knew it. But there could
be no final measuring of the mind, no ultimate testing of the spirit,
no total comprehension of the love, save as the manner of Jesus'
death completed the pattern of his life.

Had Jesus taken refuge in silence, his earlier words might have
been remembered for a while by a few, but that would have been
all. Had he sought safety in the desert, his flight might have been
regarded as natural and even sensible, but his example would
have ceased to mean anything to frightened men and women.
Had he died of natural causes, say on the evening of the first Palm
Sunday, the legend of him would have died even before the death
of his disciples.

Jesus chose to die rather than to yield; and so he held to the
straight, clear line that he had followed from the beginning. He
didn't want to die for the sake of dying: the agony he underwent
in Gethsemane proves that. But he knew he had to die, given the
situation as it was, for the sake of the life that up to then he had
taught and lived. What does the death of Jesus mean historically?
It means the historically necessary, the inevitable, the only true
completion of his life.

On these facts of history the Church proceeded to build its
faith. As the years went by, the Christian fellowship discerned
more and more of eternal meaning in the events of the years
27–29 in the life of Christ. Because the values were of infinite
importance, and because the distinctions had to be precisely made,
words were piled on words in the effort to say just what the death
of Jesus did mean in the light of eternity. Many of the words
were difficult, and some were needless; but that is of the nature
of human discourse, and it shouldn't throw us off the main track
of the quest.

It nearly did with me, when I was taking the Systematic Theology course in my own seminary. Our professor, a man with a
very formal German background and training, made us mem-
orize, with definitions, no less than seventeen distinct theories of

the atonement; and these we had to reproduce verbatim in the final examination. We students were informed, but I fear we were not much edified; and I shall not follow my old classroom outline in this section of the sermon. Rather I shall try first, and quickly, to dispose of a few common misconceptions of the Christian doctrine of the atoning death of our Lord; and then I shall attempt, and also briefly, to say what I understand the authentic and meaningful teaching to be.

The first negative is about the physical matter of the blood of Christ. "Without the shedding of blood there is no remission of sin" is a misquotation from the epistle to the Hebrews, and a complete misrepresentation of what its author was saying. His point was that blood had been essential in the sacrificial system of Judaism, but that the ideal or spiritual sacrifice (remember he was a Platonist) made such shedding of blood no longer necessary. Actually only one of our Gospel accounts of the crucifixion makes any mention of blood at all, and the amount shed even from the spear thrust could not have been great. "The blood is the life," said the ancient Jewish lawgiver, and more truly than he knew. The blood of the Christ is the very life of the Christ: the physical symbol of a spiritual reality, of a whole life poured out for the sake of mankind.

A second "No" must be said to those who hold that God could not have forgiven man's sin without the substitution of an innocent victim for the guilty. Aside from the fact that this flatly denies God's power to do as he will, it also makes the divine justice utterly unjust. God was angry at the world, says this theory; and he couldn't get over his mad till he'd taken it out on somebody—and that somebody one who hadn't caused the anger or any part of it. This is no God, but a devil; and this is no saving grace, but at best a mathematical masquerade.

It was to avoid this sort of immoral estimate of God that some of the Church Fathers, notably St. Augustine, argued that the death of our Lord was a ransom paid to the Devil. The influence here of Zoroastrian dualism will not escape you; and you will remember that St. Augustine had been a disciple of the Persian Mani before he became a Christian. If the Devil indeed were practically equal with God, then some such deal would have to be made to resolve the conflict, and to save mankind for the God of light and good. But the Persian Ahriman, as we saw a fortnight ago, doesn't have a rightful place in Christian thinking; and so a ransom paid to an autonomous Devil has no place in our thought of the atonement in Christ Jesus.

Not the blood, then; not an arbitrary satisfying of an arbitrary justice; not a payoff to a supernatural enemy of mankind. Setting these aside, what may we say in affirmation? What is the atonement we have gained by the death of the Christ? St. Paul gives us the answer, and we ought to heed him. "God was in Christ, reconciling the world unto himself." Atonement is at-one-ment: that is, precisely, reconciliation. But who is being reconciled to whom? Not God to us, O Christian people; not God to us, but we to God.

There was no need that God should love us more. He loves us, has loved us, eternally and totally. There was every need that we should love him more. But how could we love him unless we came to know him? And how could we know him until he came to live with us, not only in the likeness of our human flesh, but in the full reality of our human being?

The doctrine of the atonement therefore is none other than the doctrine of the incarnation. *Cur deus homo?* asked St. Anselm of Canterbury: Why a God-man? The death of a man who was man only could not save us: many men have died, and gallantly enough, but not to our eternal salvation. The apparition of a god who was a god only could not save us either, for still the gulf would be fixed between his nature and ours. In neither case would there be a real at-one-ment.

Deus homo, God and man united in one single personality, alone could give the answer. The Church held Jesus Christ to be both human and divine because it saw in him not only man but also God himself. It could not see the whole love of God till it saw the whole gift of love, in the man who died rather than forsake his mission and his friends. "Greater love hath no man than this . . ." Greater love has no God either; and when that man died on Calvary he made clear at last to man what true love can be, what the love of God for man is.

It is therefore a faulty separation that I have provided in this morning's outline. The theological truth of the atonement grows immediately out of the historic fact of the crucifixion; and the point of the theological teaching is and can be none other than the personal experience. Leslie asked the right question, and she phrased it exactly aright: "What does it mean when we say that Christ died to save us?"

He died to save *us:* that is just what it means. "When we were yet dead in trespasses and sins, Christ died for the ungodly." We were estranged from God, because we did not know him as he is. We knew his law, and so in our sinfulness we feared his judgment. We did not know his love, and so we could not think to accept his grace. The God-man Jesus Christ showed us at once how God may come to man, and how man himself at last may come to God. "God was in Christ, reconciling the world unto himself."

Without the ultimate sacrifice of Calvary the answer could not be complete. The author of our salvation was not complete, was not made perfect, without his suffering—without the final suffering that proved so finally his loyalty and his love. "Christ leads us through no darker rooms than he went through before." Had he not faced and endured that last testing, neither God's full love for man nor man's full capacity to love God could have been known to men.

I shall announce now, especially to Nikki Tenneson and Nancy Gilbert, that on Low Sunday, the first Sunday after Easter, I shall try to reply to their recent question about the clause in the Creed, "He descended into hell." There will be more to be said then about the intensity of agony that our Lord endured, about the hell which he entered that Heaven might be our own. As the blood is the symbol of the life poured out, so the holy cross is the summation of the glory that could come only by willing acceptance of the most awful degradation.

The preaching of the cross indeed was a stumblingblock to those who thought that goodness always brought in its train earthly success and comfort. It was foolishness to those philosophers who could not bring themselves to admit the reality of sin and suffering in the world. The preaching of the cross nevertheless is the power of God, and the wisdom of God, to those who dare to face the facts of life. The Christian message of salvation by the cross is the one Gospel that relates at once the immediate fact to the ultimate truth, and the ultimate truth again to actual human need. What does the death of Jesus mean? It means real salvation in a real world: and there is no other way whereby man can be saved from his sins and from himself.

Jesus died to save us. He had to die, or he would have been saved at our expense. He had to be crucified, or we could not have known the nature of love in its fullness. He had to choose to die, or we would not have learned how we may choose to live. God was in Christ: no one, knowing the Master, could doubt that. God, in Christ, was reconciling the world unto himself: no one, knowing the world, can suppose we might be reconciled to God in any easier way.

It was for human sin that Jesus died: and so it is for human salvation that his death remains the one oblation once offered, a full, perfect, and sufficient sacrifice for the sins of the whole world. That is what it means, Leslie and all the rest of you. But remember that, though Jesus our Lord died to save us, he saves none of us who are not willing to be saved. God was in Christ, reconciling the world unto himself. Are we ready to be reconciled to God?

Did Jesus Go to Hell?

"Low Sunday," 25 April 1954. Psalm 66:1, 14–18; Jeremiah 15:10–21; St. Luke 22:37–46.

* * *

He descended into hell.—The Apostles' Creed.

Now that he ascended, what is it but that he also descended first into the lower parts of the earth? He that descended is the same also that ascended up far above all heavens.—Ephesians 4:9f.

The Lord set his cross in the midst of hell, which is the sign of victory: and it shall remain there for ever.—ACTS OF PILATE, fourth century after Christ.

One Sunday noon at coffee Nikki Tenneson and Nancy Gilbert, who evidently had been discussing the subject, came to me with a question. "Why," they asked, "do we say in the Creed, 'He descended into hell'?" This morning offered the first opening in our spring schedule for a chance to reply in any detail; and this Low Sunday, a week after Easter Day, provides an appropriate time for us to go back and consider some of the factors that made Easter possible.

In this peculiarly happy religious situation in which we live at Mills, where we seek to be "thoroughly Christian but not sectarian," few of us know or think anything about anyone else's particular denominational background. As Chaplain I do have a "religious preference" list which is supplied to me by the Office of Record, but I make practically no use of it in connection with our Chapel activities. Today, however, I'm going to spot my two

169

questioners denominationally, because their respective Church connections bear directly on their approaches to their question.

Nikki is a Methodist, and Nancy is a Presbyterian. The statement, "He descended into hell," stands today in the official Presbyterian service book, but not in the Methodist one. And so it would seem that Nancy is supposed to descend into hell, but Nikki isn't.

But the story is a lot more complicated than that. John Wesley, who founded the Methodist Church without having intended to do anything of the sort, left the clause in the Creed when he adapted the Church of England prayer book for the use of his American followers; but the Methodists in America saw fit to vote it out. In the first *Book of Common Worship* of the American Presbyterians, published in 1906, there was a footnote to our sentence which read, "*i.e.*, he continued in the state of the dead, and under the power of death, until the third day." In 1932 the revised Presbyterian book cut that to read only, "He continued in the state of the dead until the third day." The most recent edition, that of 1946, has dropped the footnote altogether.

Nor was it only in Methodist and Presbyterian circles that some difficulty was felt. The first prayer book of the Protestant Episcopal Church, which was issued in 1789, said that the congregation might say, "He went into the place of departed spirits," or might just leave the troublesome clause unsaid. That latter permission was removed in 1892; but, as you can see from the books we have been using this morning, there is still the rubric on page 15:

And any Churches may, instead of the words, He descended into hell, *use the words,* He went into the place of departed spirits, *which are considered as words of the same meaning in the Creed.*

So far as I know, no one ever does use the eight words instead of the four, which would mean twelve syllables instead of seven; but the permission to do so stands as witness that the reference to hell has been bothersome to American Episcopalians, as well as to members of other denominations, for at least 165 years.

In order to clear the decks, we ought first to talk about hell and its nature. Just what did, what does, that word "hell" mean? The Presbyterian "state of the dead," and the Episcopal "place of departed spirits," both point toward one correct answer. The Hebrew word *Sheol* is translated as "hell" thirty-one times in the King James Old Testament; but it appears in exactly an equal number of times as "the grave," and three times as "the pit." This suggests what is the fact; namely, that Sheol was not the fiery hell of torment of which commonly we think, but only a shadowy abode of all the dead, thought of without moral distinction between sinners and the righteous, and without any consideration of punishment or reward.

This clearly is what the theologians of our modern Churches had in mind when they were trying to interpret, and so appeared to be softening, the flat statement, "He descended into hell." Surely, they seem to have thought, it was inconceivable that our sinless Lord had been committed to a hell of punishment, to anything like the *Inferno* of Dante Alighieri. They took refuge, therefore, in the legitimate meaning of the Hebrew Sheol, and suggested that what the Creed declares is only that Jesus was really dead.

This is all right as far as it goes. The point was made explicitly, about A.D. 210, by the Latin Christian lawyer Tertullian:

Though Christ is God, because he was man also, he died according to the scriptures, and in accordance with the same was buried. With this same law he complied by remaining in the form of a dead man in the underworld; nor did he ascend into the heights of the heavens, until he had descended into the inner parts of the earth.

Thus also at the end of the fourth century Rufinus of Aquileia, commenting upon just this clause in the Creed, argued:

The divine nature descended into death by the flesh, not that under the law of mortals it should be held by death, but that being raised by itself it should open the doors of death.

Much of the purpose of the Apostles' Creed, as gradually it was taking form from the second century to the sixth, was to distinguish the standard Christian position from the aberrant views of heretics. In particular it was directed against the heresy called Gnosticism, which tended to deny not at all our Lord's divinity, but precisely his true humanity. As early as A.D. 117 St. Ignatius of Smyrna had cautioned his readers:

Do not listen . . . when anyone speaks to you apart from Jesus Christ, who truly was born from the seed of David, and from Mary; who ate and drank; who truly suffered under Pontius Pilate, truly was crucified, and died.

This then is the first reply to this morning's question. All men must die, and must go to whatever may be the state of the dead. It is essential to the true Christian doctrine of Jesus' full humanity that he should not have escaped any element in universal human experience; and so it was necessary that he should die, as shall we, and should enter in his own person into the place of departed spirits.

But physical death is not the whole story, and neither is the vague and undifferentiated Sheol of early Hebrew thinking. Good and evil, men realized increasingly, were different one from the other. Different also were sorrow and joy, and different were pleasure and pain. These distinctions, so evidently real in man's present life, surely were too real to be wiped out by the single instant of one's physical dying. And so little by little Jewish thinking, no doubt with the aid of considerable influence from Persia, moved toward the concepts we know respectively as those of Paradise and Hell.

The late Jewish word for "hell," however, belonged first to an actual place in this world, and one indeed on the very edge of the city of Jerusalem. It appears in recent English versions of the New Testament as "Gehenna." The Hebrew form, in two words, was *Ge Hinnom*, "the valley of Hinnom." This was a deep cleft on the south side of the city, around the southeastern corner of the wall from the valley of the Kidron; and from long before the time of Jesus this declivity had served as the Jerusalem city dump.

There were fires burning continually there, as always man has used fire to get rid of his rubbish. Some of the Jewish writings of the New Testament period, such as the book of Enoch and the so-called IV Ezra, contain vivid descriptions of the flames of Gehenna, which consumed everything that was cast into them. But the essential character of a dump is not the burning of waste materials: it is the fact of waste itself. And the critical element in the identifying of Gehenna, and so of "hell" within this frame of thought, is not so much the melodrama of man's punishment after death as it is the awful tragedy of a wasted life.

Did Jesus go to this kind of hell? Did he find himself in Gehenna? Actually he and his friends must have walked past the physical Gehenna, the valley of Hinnom, that first Maundy Thursday evening on their way from the last supper to the garden of Gethsemane. From the pathway on the city wall they had looked down upon the dots of flame, and had caught the stench of all the rotten stuff that the city had thrown away. Waste, rubbish, spoilage—all that man had no further use for— all this had been thrown into Gehenna.

On they walked, down from the wall, through the Kidron bottom, and up the little slope into Gethsemane. There Jesus knelt alone and wrestled with his fate, with himself, with his God. Waste? What else had been all the years of the ministry? No one really had caught the meaning of the divine love as he had tried to reveal it. Rubbish? Didn't even Peter and James and John think so? How else could they be lying there snoring now, a stone's cast down the hill? What man had no use for? How better describe the message that even now was bringing Judas and the soldiers to arrest him?

Oh, yes, Jesus did go to hell. He was deep down in Gehenna that evening in the garden. Thirty years of living, almost three years of active teaching, all down the drain into the sewer. Waste; rubbish; discard. The world didn't want him, had no understanding of him, was determined to thrust him out of further sight. All was lost. Why not give up, climb the little hill of Olivet, and escape down the steep slope to the Jordan Valley? His sweat was as it were great drops of blood falling down to the ground.

Our Lord would not have been truly man, could not have entered fully into man's experience, had he not known this hell of seeing his life as wasted and himself as rubbish. There can be no hell worse than this: and ever and again, in our living, each of us enters into this worst Gehenna of seeing himself as useless to man and to God. What the Gospel story tells us, and what our Creed summarizes for us in its four simple words, is just that Jesus went through the worst that man can know; and that he not only went through it, but came through it with his faith undimmed and his loyalty untarnished.

Had he not endured this Gehenna of the human soul, and at this its absolute worst, our Lord could not be for us a sufficient example and a sufficient Saviour. The captain of our salvation, says the writer to the Hebrews, was made perfect through sufferings. And the real suffering, the most fearful agony, was not the pain of the body on the cross, but the torment of the spirit that came before.

Nikki, you and I will have to admit that the Methodists have been fearfully wrong in erasing these four words from the Creed. Only if we know how far our Lord descended into hell, shall we have any understanding of how and why he could ascend into heaven and take his place at the right hand of God. Without the cross there could be no resurrection, and without Gehenna there can be no Paradise. This was true of Jesus, and it is true for us. Let us never forget it as we say this little, simple, and infinitely meaningful sentence in our declaration of our Christian faith.

There was yet another meaning that the Church, again very early, gave to the descent of the Lord into the lower regions.

Here we turn once more to the Hebrew idea of Sheol, and its Greek equivalent called "Hades," as the shadowy abode of all the dead. In such a place, in such a meaningless and joyless condition, were supposed to be all who had died in all the ages. Included among them, then, were all the heroes of Old Testament days, the very builders of the faith in which Jesus had grown up and in which Christianity had its deepest roots.

The Church believed that only in its Lord Jesus Christ could there be salvation for any man or woman. What then about those who never had had the chance to hear of the Christ? What of those who had lived and died long centuries before Jesus was born?

The formal doctrine of Christian exclusiveness yielded, and very soon, to a sense of fundamental fairness. Surely some means had to be found to take care of the worthies of old time, and to provide for them a share in the glory of the Christ's eternal kingdom. The device which was used belonged to the thinking of that age, but the motive and the meaning have relevance in all the ages that have been and are to be.

Some of you have seen, in the European cathedrals, those tremendous paintings and bas-reliefs of "the harrowing of hell." They relate to just this problem, and they depend upon the view that Jesus went into Hades in the interim between his death and his rising again. The thought now, however, is not of his own suffering, but of his offering salvation to all those who till now had had no chance of it.

Behind the pictures stand such vivid imaginations as that of the fourth century writer of the *Acts of Pilate*. Let us hear him speak, in the latter part of his story. (For the sake of any academic purists who may be listening, I shall tell you that I have combined here two versions of the text, one the Greek and the other one known as "Latin B." But I assure you that there is no disharmony between them.)

Then the Lord Jesus, the Saviour of all men, pitiful and most

gracious, greeted Adam with kindness, saying unto him: Peace be
unto thee, Adam, and unto thy children unto everlasting ages.
Then Father Adam cast himself at the Lord's feet, and rose up and
kissed his hands, and shed abundant tears, saying . . . Thou art come,
O King of glory, to set men free and gather them to thine everlasting
kingdom. Then our mother Eve also in like manner cast herself at
the feet of the Lord, and rose up and kissed his hands, and shed
tears abundantly, and said: Behold the hands which fashioned me:
testifying unto all.

Likewise also all the prophets and the saints said: We give thanks
unto thee, O Christ, Saviour of the world, for that thou has brought
up our life from corruption. And when they had thus said, the
Saviour blessed Adam upon his forehead with the sign of the cross,
and so did he also unto all the patriarchs and prophets and martyrs
and forefathers. And he took them and leaped up out of hell. And
as he went the holy fathers sang praises, following him and saying:
Blessed is he that cometh in the Name of the Lord. Unto him be
the glory of all the saints.

Then all the saints of God besought the Lord that he would leave
the sign of victory—even of the holy cross—in hell, that the wicked
ministers thereof might not prevail to keep back any that was ac-
cused, whom the Lord absolved. And so it was done, and the Lord
set his cross in the midst of hell, which is the sign of victory; and
it shall remain there for ever. Then all we went out thence with
the Lord, and left Satan and Hell in Tartarus.

No, the imagery is not ours: but surely the meaning and the
value are for us, and for all people. What these early Christians
were declaring was their profound and triumphant faith that no
one is outside the power of the divine salvation. Wherever and
whenever they lived, whatever their fate and fortune may have
been, they may know the love of God in Christ Jesus reaching
out to them. "He descended into hell." Into whatever hell he
may have to go to find us, the Lord of our salvation goes to bring
up our life from corruption. This is what the Church believed;
and in its sharing of the divine love it could not think that any
of the children of God were to be left outside the scope of the
divine mercy.

We thank you, Nikki and Nancy, for bringing up one of the most important questions of our Chapel year. Four little words: and yet they say these mighty things, they teach these lessons of eternal import. "He descended into hell." Why do we say this in the Creed?

We say it first because we believe not only that Jesus was indeed a human being in our human world, but also that he entered into the deepest valley of human despair, and so that he is able to lead us out of our own despairing. We say it also because we believe that God's salvation in Christ Jesus is for all mankind, in every time and every land. Still, and always, the Lord says in his mercy, "Peace be unto thee, Adam, and unto thy children unto everlasting ages."

Now that he ascended, what is it but that he also descended into the lowest parts of human living? The Lord set his cross in the midst of hell, which is the sign of victory: and it shall remain there for ever.

He descended into hell. Then all we may go out thence with the Lord.

Is There Health in Us?

2 May 1954, at the Holy Communion. I St. Peter 2:19–25; St. John 10:11–16.

*   *   *

We have done those things which we ought not to have done; And there is no health in us. But thou, O Lord, have mercy upon us, miserable offenders.—The General Confession at Morning and Evening Prayer, 1552 and after.

I know that in me (that is, in my flesh,) dwelleth no good thing: for to will is present with me; but how to perform that which is good I find not. . . . O wretched man that I am! who shall deliver me from the body of this death?—Romans 7:18, 24.

By another of those interesting coincidences which occur so often, two inquiries about difficult expressions in our regular order of service came to me almost simultaneously a couple of months ago. One, the question from Nikki Tenneson and Nancy Gilbert about the statement in the Creed, "He descended into hell," we considered last Sunday. Today we turn to a question from Ann Hawkes about another puzzling clause, this time one in the General Confession at Morning Prayer.

Mrs. Hawkes tells me that her late husband, the distinguished Dean Hawkes of Columbia College, never would say in the Columbia chapel service the words "and there is no health in us." I gather that he insisted, with a healthy independence of mind, that there was health anyway in him; and he would not commit what seemed to him to be the dishonesty of declaring that there wasn't. Akin to this, and even more common, is an objection many people make to calling themselves "miserable offenders": including a few who are regular attendants at our services here. Are we indeed miserable offenders? Is there any health in us? Those questions merit careful analysis; and we must analyze very carefully before we can hope to reply accurately.

The Confession which includes these debatable and much debated words was a new contribution of Archbishop Thomas Cranmer and his associates to the Prayer Book of 1552. In the earlier book, that of 1549, both Matins and Evensong began with the Lord's Prayer, and neither service included any confession of sins. Since the 1552 book bore many marks of Puritan influence, it may be supposed that it was on Puritan insistence that a penitential introduction to the service was prefixed to its former beginning. There was historic precedent for it, however, in a mutual confession of sins between minister and choir in the medieval monastic services of Prime in the morning and Compline in the evening.

Neither our Morning Prayer confession, nor that which we shall be using in a few minutes in the Communion office, was a translation from existing Latin texts. Both were new compositions of the English reformers, and both were derived very obviously from the words of scripture. The basis for that at Morning Prayer is the analysis of human sinfulness in the seventh chapter of St. Paul's letter to the Romans, in which is included our second text for today: "I know that in me (that is, in my flesh,) dwelleth no good thing."

Mr. Hawkes's distaste for what seemed to him an extreme and unjustified self-condemnation clearly has been shared by many others, including a number of people in authority in our Churches. John Wesley left the Confession as it was in the Church of England service, but the Methodist Church in America has cut from the text both the clause "there is no health in us" and the words "miserable offenders." So also have the American Congregationalists, in their *Book of Worship* of 1948. In *Christian Worship: A Service Book*, edited by Professor G. E. Osborn of Phillips University for the Disciples of Christ in 1953, "miserable offenders" is left out but "there is no health in us" remains in the text.

The American Presbyterians, on the other hand, stand with the Episcopalians on this matter as last Sunday we saw that they do with reference to "he descended into hell." Both in the Presbyterian *Book of Common Worship* of 1932 and in that of 1946 the Confession appears exactly as it has in all the Anglican books for the past four centuries. For completeness of record, it should be said that the Lutherans, whose tradition comes from Germany rather than from England, do not use this particular form of confession; but that their service opens with a brief confession to the effect that "we poor sinners . . . are by nature sinful and unclean."

As I did last week, so again today I shall take my stand with the Anglicans, the Presbyterians, and John Wesley, in favor of the original text, and so in opposition to the deletions made by the modern Methodists and the Congregationalists. But I owe it to both Deans Hawkes, and to all of you, to try to tell you why.

I said "modern Methodists" with deliberate intent. Perhaps I should have said "modernist Methodists." The reluctance to declare the essential sinfulness of man reflects what was called the "modernist" movement in practically all the Protestant Churches of a generation ago. This was really one aspect of the general attitude of optimism about man and the world which came out of late nineteenth century prosperity and early twentieth century technological success.

Dean Hawkes will understand me when I say that there was no more notable academic representative of this mood than Columbia University. That great institution's gallant defense of individual freedom (today being so ably carried on by President Grayson Kirk), its faith in humanity, its daring in educational and social experiment, changed the whole face of American thinking. That such a healthy man as Herbert Hawkes, living in and helping to create so healthy an environment, should repudiate the notion that there was "no health in him" is in no way surprising. We respect his self-respect, and I admire his honesty. But there are some of us who can not share his apparent optimism about human nature in general; and we must observe that the Church has not accepted it either, except in just the halcyon years in which Dean Hawkes lived and worked.

Have you ever thought about the absolute realism of the prayers set forth in the *Book of Common Prayer*? Nowadays we take too many of them symbolically or allegorically, and therefore much too foggily. When in the Litany the English of 1549 prayed for deliverance "from all sedition, privy conspiracy, and rebellion," they were thinking directly of plots against the new Protestant régime; and they followed this petition with one which Queen Elizabeth I wisely ordered deleted when she came to the throne: "From the tyranny of the Bishop of Rome, and all his detestable enormities, good Lord, deliver us."

Similarly when in the Collect for Peace we beseech Almighty God to "defend us thy humble servants in all assaults of our enemies . . . that we may not fear the power of any adversaries," the reference is not to mere personal quarrels, and still less to vaguely conceived forces of spiritual evil. When the Pope Gelasius wrote the prayer, late in the fifth century, he had in mind the still continuing threat of the northern barbarians. When the English reformers translated it in the middle of the sixteenth century they surely were looking down the Bay of Biscay toward Spain, whose crown prince as Philip II soon was to marry the English princess Mary, and who less than forty years later was to send his great Armada against the English coasts.

Remember that next Sunday when our familiar Collect is read. The plea is above all for peace in the heart; but its context still is that of a world which is not at peace, and its reference for us is most patently to those very actual powers of this present world—yes, I do mean Russia and her supporters—who threaten at once the peace of nations and that of our own spirits. The Prayer Book was put together by real people in a real world; and its realism challenges us always to live our religion actually in a world of actuality.

But if the Prayer Book is thus realistic, the Holy Scriptures upon which it depended are not less so; and our General Confession in particular is a Prayer Book catena of materials from the New Testament. If Gelasius was factual about the barbarians, and Cranmer about privy conspiracy (remember that a political overturn consigned him to be burned at the stake just four years after his second prayer book had appeared), the apostle Paul was not less factual about the inherent sinfulness of the human heart.

"I know that in me (that is, in my flesh,) dwelleth no good thing: . . . O wretched man that I am! who shall deliver me from the body of this death?" The doctrine of original sin is no arbitrary construct upon the myth of Adam and Eve. It is rather the expression of a frank and penetrating insight into the nature of the human animal. Without any awareness of biological evolution, the early theologians—and we must count among them, long before St. Paul, the writer of the fifty-first Psalm—the early theologians saw the brutal selfishness, the selfish cowardice, the alternating arrogance and fear that marked what we know as the most complex of the primates, *Homo* often miscalled *sapiens*.

What led to *Homo* being called *sapiens*, however—what made man seem to be wise, at least relatively speaking—was that he had shown a capacity for rising now and then above his animal nature and bringing it under a measure of control. Many will say, and the liberal modernists did say emphatically, that this was a matter of education—or, to use a Columbia University word, one of socialization. This, so far as it goes, I will not deny. As an educator I believe in education, and as a sociologist I am all for the socializing of our greedy, grasping, self-seeking selves.

But as a Christian I must go on to say that education and socialization are instrumental processes; and in philosophy I do not share the view that the instrument is to be seen as the ultimate reality. The first major reality in our problem is our sinfulness. The other reality, and the crucial one for our being saved from ourselves, is the grace of God. Man may educate and socialize, and under God's will he must. But only God himself can save us, only God can give us either motive for education or power to use it aright.

This surely is much more evident in these tragic times of ours than it was in the heyday of liberal modernism. We have solved neither our world problems nor those of our own daily living. Envy, avarice, sloth, pride, the lusts of the flesh: the seven deadly sins are as rampant among us as ever they were in pagan Rome or renaissance Europe. The technology that produced the H bomb has failed utterly to produce good sense in mankind, let alone good will. Our confession is general, one for all of us sinners; and both corporately and individually we all know how deeply we have sinned, how far we have come short of the glory of God. There is no health in *us*.

I suppose, to make the statement in our Confession explicitly clear, we ought to phrase it, "there is no moral health in our animal natures." But we are precisely our animal natures, and nothing else, save as God's own life is breathed into our beings. And the remainder of the Confession makes it evident that the outcome we seek from a full confession of our wrongness is that God shall set us aright:

But thou, O Lord, have mercy upon us miserable offendors. [In the book of 1552 there was no comma after "us."] Spare thou them, O God, which confesse theyr faultes. Restore thou them that be penitent, according to thy promyses declared unto mankynde, in Christe Jesu oure Lorde. And graunt, O most merciful father, for his sake, that we may hereafter live a godly, righteous, and sobre life, to the glory of thy holy name. Amen.

Union Theological Seminary is practically a part of Columbia University; and one suspects it is not an accident that Union today is the American fountainhead of a Christian theology which has recovered the Reformation mood in its realizing that man never can lift himself by his own bootstraps. The fact of sin can be countered only by the fact of God. Many will not escape from his sin save as he recognizes it in himself, and as he confesses it to the eternal Father who alone can save.

In me (that is, in my flesh) dwelleth no good thing. There is no health in me, the animal descendant of the Hedleys and the Whiteheads, and before them of the animals swinging from tree to tree. I am by my nature a miserable offender. God grant that I shall not forget this. In so far as I remember it, but only so far, I am ready to receive the grace of God to rise above it.

We confess our sins, and our sinfulness, that we may be saved from them by God in Jesus Christ. Who shall deliver me from the body of this death? God will.

CONCLUDING: FOR SENIORS

The End of All Things

The End of All Things

30 May 1954, at the last Sunday morning service before
Degree Day. Psalm 93; Daniel 7:15–28; I St. Peter 4:7–11.

*   *   *

*The end of all things is at hand: be ye therefore sober, and
watch unto prayer.*—I St. Peter 4:7.

We may not think that the writer of this little letter of the
late first century after Christ had Mills College specifically in
mind. Nor is it reasonable to suppose that the compiler of the
late sixth century lectionary of Würzburg, which is our earliest
authority for the fixing of our passage from I St. Peter as the
Epistle for this Sunday before Pentecost, was thinking about
either our Examination Week or our approaching Degree Day.
Historically and statistically, we shall have to put the coincidence down to—well, coincidence. Morally, however, we may
find it possible to take another view.

In one way you who are Seniors must have felt that the real
"end of all things" came upon you in the Comprehensives Friday
and yesterday; and your classmates who this morning are relax-
ing down at Carmel are but dramatizing the calm after the
storm, the sudden escape after four years of hard labor and many
recent weeks of mounting tension. There are other emotional
stresses yet before you, nevertheless: the parade down from
Pinetop with your lanterns on Thursday evening, and your singing of "Goodbye, friends, we leave you"; the last meal all together on Friday morning, with President and Mrs. White as
your gracious hosts; and the Commencement program of a week
from this afternoon, whose beauty and dignity traditionally

187

finish, after the solemn academic procession of the faculty has filed out of the Greek Theater, with one terrific yell of triumph and release as all at once the Seniors realize that at long last they have become alumnae.

The end of all things? Sometimes it seems that here at Mills we take an unconscionable time really to arrive at the end. But that too is the way that life usually takes—as we shall see in our examining now the two passages from the Bible that have been read in this service.

Let us look first at the seventh chapter of this strange book of Daniel. The setting is that of political turmoil in the second century B.C. The "fourth beast" in this chapter, specified as representing a "fourth kingdom," is the world empire of Alexander the Great, which had succeeded and had far surpassed the earlier régimes of the Babylonians, the (more or less mythical) Medes, and the Persians. The "ten horns," or "ten kings," are the successor monarchs of the Seleucid dynasty of Syrian Antioch, which exercised power in varying degrees from 312 B.C. to 66 B.C. The other and "diverse" king, who thinks "to change times and laws," is Antiochus Epiphanes, the persecutor of the Jews who attempted to abolish their sacred festivals.

"A time and times and the dividing of time" may not have meant much to you when I read the phrase in the lesson. It is commonly understood to signify "a year, two years, and half a year," and to refer to three and a half years of special attack by Antiochus upon Jewish custom and faith. Then the end, said this writer, really would come; and the everlasting dominion would "be given to the people of the saints of the most High."

If we turn to the end of this same book of Daniel, however, we shall see that the ending was not quite so easy, nor so complete, as our author had anticipated. In Chapter 12, Verse 7, we find the three years and a half mentioned again, but in 12:11 we have "a thousand two hundred and ninety days," which is a little longer. Then comes 12:12, which reads, "Blessed is he that waiteth, and cometh to the thousand three hundred and five and thirty days," or yet another forty-five days added. And finally, in the very last verse of the book, either the first author or a slightly later editor gives up on the chronology altogether, and advises: "But go thou thy way till the end be: for thou shalt rest, and stand in thy lot at the end of the days."

We know now that there was for the Jews of the second century B.C. no such final triumph as these gallantly hopeful dreamers envisaged. The sons of Mattathias, known as the Maccabees, did defeat Antiochus and set up an independent Jewish kingdom. It fell far short, however, of being a Messianic world dominion, and after just a hundred years it was swallowed up in the relentless expansion of Rome. All the characters of the second century drama had long passed from the scene, and the end was not yet.

Two and a half centuries afterward, the early Christians went through an almost identical sequence of hopeful thinking and disillusioning experience. The Church was convinced that Jesus of Nazareth was the true Messiah, so long and so eagerly expected by the Jewish people. But the historic Jesus had not set his nation free from oppression, had not overthrown the empire of Rome, had not set up a kingdom of his own upon the earth. In fact, he had not even begun to achieve as much politically as had the Maccabees two centuries before. Taxed with this glaring discrepancy between the obvious facts and the Christian claim that Jesus was the Messiah, the Church quickly answered by saying, in effect, "Well, perhaps not yet, but surely very soon." Thus there arose, quite possibly with some support from Jesus' own acceptance of Jewish hopes for a final, all-changing cataclysm, the Christian expectation that the Lord soon would return in spectacular power, and put an end to the long centuries in which sin and suffering had dominated the life of man.

This was part of the standard Christian message as it was given to St. Paul in his own Christian indoctrination. Accepting it at

face value, the new apostle to the Gentiles had to work it out
for himself in experimental detail because the people in the
Church of Thessalonica (our modern Saloniki) got worried because some of their number had died before the Lord's promised
appearance. "We which are alive and remain," he assured them,

shall not prevent [that is, "come before"] them which are asleep. For
the Lord himself shall descend from heaven with a shout, with the
voice of the archangel, and with the trump of God: and the dead
in Christ shall rise first: then we which are alive and remain shall be
caught up together with them in the clouds, to meet the Lord in
the air: and so shall we ever be with the Lord.

Not long afterward, however, in a second letter to these same
people of Saloniki, St. Paul found himself driven to change his
emphasis. In II Thessalonians he drew upon Daniel and other
Jewish writings of the period to explain why the end had not
come yet, and could not come at any easily predictable time.
"Comfort your hearts," he told them, "and stablish you in every
good word and work." In the same context we hear him warning
those who had laid aside their daily occupations in order to wait
for the Lord: "If a man will not work, neither let him eat."

From this time on, so far as we know from his surviving letters, the apostle said nothing explicit about this difficult problem.
He focused his attention rather upon the issues of life in this
present world, and devoted himself to urging the claims of personal Christian faith, character, and conduct, in the midst of an
alien and largely hostile setting. At the last we find him writing, to the young Timothy, "I am now ready to be offered, and
the time of my departure is at hand." (The time of his own departure, note; not at all that of the Lord's return to earth.)

I have fought a good fight, I have finished my course, I have kept
the faith: Henceforth there is laid up for me a crown of righteousness,
which the Lord, the righteous judge, shall give me at that day.

But though St. Paul seems thus to have modified his thought

about the approaching "end of all things," the Church as a whole did not lightly surrender its expectation. This so-called first letter of St. Peter seems actually to be the work of an unknown Christian in Asia Minor, and to have been written during the sharp persecution under the Emperor Domitian in the year 96. Even then, more than thirty years after St. Paul had died for his faith, hope deferred had not become hope abandoned. Still the stubborn dream persisted, and still the harried believers were told in perfect confidence, "The end of all things is at hand."

It is evident to us, often appallingly evident, that all these worthies of old time were mistaken. The end did not come in 164 B.C., nor in A.D. 50, nor in A.D. 96. Neither did it come in the year 1000, which many in that later day thought would be a really tidy time for the winding up of the world's story. The end has not come yet, and the Lord's kingdom looks to be as far as ever from being established upon the earth. In all the centuries since Daniel there have been those who have made war with the saints, who have spoken great words against the most High, who have sought to wear out the saints of the most High. No Messianic kingdom has been given to us; and as we look at this world of ours in 1954 we scarcely can think that one is likely to be.

The writer of the book of Daniel was wrong, then. So also was St. Paul, at least in the earlier years of his ministry. And so was the author of I St. Peter, whoever he may have been. Shall we then set their works aside, as childish imaginings that have no relevance to our own realistic, scientific, hard-bitten approach to life? Before we do, let us pause to think of them, and with them, just a few minutes more. There is more than chronology involved here. There is faith in God, and there is challenge to men.

Why was the book of Daniel written at all? Why but to call the Jews to maintain their loyalty in their ancient faith, despite all manner of present tribulation? Why did St. Paul seek to encourage the Thessalonians? His answer is explicit: "that no man should be moved by these afflictions." What does I St. Peter say about the duty of man in view of the expected end? "Be ye therefore sober, and watch unto prayer."

We cannot accept the chronology, and we do not expect the cataclysm. But we shall fare badly if we think therefore to reject the challenge. Whenever and whatever the end may be, whether or not there is to be ever any ending at all, our job is here and now. All the stories about the brave young Daniel are designed to call the Jewish people to follow their hero in perduring devotion to the God of their fathers. All the stress of St. Paul is upon the fruits of the Spirit in "love, joy, peace, longsuffering, gentleness, goodness, faith." All the drive of I St. Peter is to the end that the people called Christian shall be "holy in all manner of conversation," and that they shall "take it patiently" when they "do well, and suffer for it."

But why? What is the motivation, if that of the approaching end is to be set aside? The answer is not in the end, but in the continuum: in the everlasting purpose of the eternal God. These men of old guessed wrong about time and times and half-times. But they weren't guessing about—they were apprehending by faith—the backdrop and the groundwork of their temporary and inaccurate expectations. What they believed in, basically, was no more and no less than God's being, God's wisdom, God's righteousness, God's total and eternal power.

Here, and here alone, we shall find what we need if we are to hold a steady course amid the tempests and the crosscurrents of our voyage through life. Only in God may we know stability. Only by God's will can we guide our lives aright. Only by God's grace shall we endure to whatever may be the end for us. This is the essence, and this is the summation, of the Hebrew-Christian faith. This is the tested and single answer to the question of how men and women may be true to themselves when all the world turns false to them.

Seniors of 1954, the end of all things is not yet. It was an inspired inconsistency that first called a graduation ceremony a "Commencement." All in life is beginning, and all is ending, because all in life is continuation. You secured admission here at Mills, and that was a fresh start for you after prep school. But you started again with each new year, each new semester, each new course. As each of these ended, you went on to something different; but it too proved to be much the same, and in its turn it came out, as the popular phrase expresses it, with the "same difference."

As of yesterday you're done with your Comprehensives. It's still a week till you'll be alumnae. And that ending will be but the prelude to your marriage or your new job or your years of graduate study. Each of those will continue, with each ending beginning a fresh ending, and each beginning ending in yet another beginning. Fifty years of this you have ahead of you, the insurance actuaries say. The end of all things is at hand? No, not just yet. Not ever.

Can you keep on through it all? Can you take this forthcoming B.A. or B.S. of yours, and then leave it alone? Can you bear to find out that each victory is only the start of a new and a harder campaign? Can you accept defeat as the call to strive again, and even harder, for the triumph you know you'll never quite win? That is the way human life has been and is and will be.

The end of all things? Goodbye, now, you dear ones. We have no fears for you, because we believe you have the root of the matter in you. End or no end, you are called to be sober and to watch unto prayer. Yours it is to seek the will of God for you, and to obey it in all the years that are to be. You will not be moved by the all too visible afflictions of this visible world, if you have learned to endure as seeing Him who is invisible.

Here is the benediction to you, in words from this same old letter that bears the name of St. Peter:

The God of all grace, who hath called us unto his eternal glory by Christ Jesus, after that ye have suffered a while, make you perfect, stablish, strengthen, settle you.

Not only after you suffer, but while you suffer, God is your refuge and strength, a very present help in trouble. Therefore you will not fear, whether or not the earth be removed. God bless and keep you. God see you through, to the end of all things and far, far beyond it.